HE
HAD
TO
GO
THERE

HE HAD TO GO THERE

The Multicultural Mandate

"If there was ever a time to go there, it is now..."

Pastor Rae Orozco

When God said "GO!" it was followed by one of the most inclusive words I know—"ALL." A true understanding and response to the diversity in the church that God himself has orchestrated have often evaded the modern-day church.
In response to an obvious Kingdom mandate, Pastor Rae has managed to produce a transcript of Kingdom magnitude. She has skillfully captured candor with care in such a way that challenges readers to both respond to the compelling call to personally reflect while embracing the equally persuasive call to go to ALL. The heart of the Father is for every race, class, creed, or gender. Thank you for your obedience, my friend.

—Dr. Kenroy Burke
Bishop, New Testament Church of God, Barbados

While reading the book, my mind went to Revelations 7:9: "After this I looked, and behold, a great multitude that no one could number, from every nation, from all tribes and peoples and languages, standing before the throne and before the Lamb, clothed in white robes, with palm branches in their hands." Pastor Rae's book will cause you to consider that this should not just be a picture of Heaven, but a picture of His church here on earth as well. Instead of Sunday mornings being the most segregated time and place, what if we took to heart the mandate to love each other and be a united church? *He Had to Go There* will certainly challenge us to move beyond our comfort and tradition and really delve into the example that Jesus set for us in loving the unlovable, befriending the outcast, and giving bread of life to those we deemed unworthy.

—Yvette Santana
Regional Women's Director
Church of God Southwestern Hispanic Region

Pastor Rae Orozco has made a significant contribution to the church in this book, *He Had to Go There*. The Great Commission compels us as a church to go into all the world and make disciples—that is our mission. Fulfilling that mission is impossible without an understanding of the multicultural mandate of the Bible as modeled in the ministry of Jesus. The world has come to our doorstep. The mission fields are now our surrounding neighborhoods. How does a local church reach the world that is next door to us? That is the question. This is a textbook on *why* and *how* a local church should and can have a multicultural ministry.

Born out of her personal experience in growing and leading a multicultural congregation, Pastor Rae's book will serve as a strategic plan that will assist a pastor in reaching their community with the Gospel.

Christ's multicultural mandate is at the heart of our mission as a church—we must go there!

—Bishop Mitchell Corder
Director, Church Health and Revitalization
Church of God International

Rae Orozco has boldly drilled down to tackle an issue that's kept the church from fulfilling its greatest Kingdom potential. She shines a scriptural light on the Kingdom importance of diversity in the body of Christ and the value that we must hold in our hearts for one another in order to see the true expression of the Kingdom of God in the earth. This book is a must-read!

—Pastor Travis Hall
Lead pastor, Life International Church (Atlanta)
Author of 7 Deadly Thoughts

Dr. Orozco offers a credible "must-read" challenge for anyone interested in making a difference in the global conversation on multiculturalism. *He Had to Go There* engages historical and theological perspectives intertwined with stories that keep readers on the edge of their seats. The work is not merely a book but rather a timeless resource fit for the libraries of the most serious of Christian apologists. Orozco exposes the inconsistency of Christian orthodoxy and orthopraxy as it relates to the Great Commission. Learn from one of the best and most authentic leaders as she presents a powerful and prophetic call to action.

—Dr. Marion Ingegneri

Professor, Life Pacific University and LifePoint Christian University

Founding pastor, Grace North Network of Churches, Arizona International Church of the Foursquare Gospel

It was with sincere joy receiving the news of Pastor Rae's new book. She is a profound, prolific, and life-changing champion leader, with extraordinary insight into the Word, the subject of diversity, and the epitome of multiculturalism. Her book is a game-changer and will be a paradigm shift for many. We salute her for sharing her kingdom insight and mantling in this area. We are blessed to call our sister, and our friend.

—Apostle Jessie and Pastor Chauntell West

Senior leaders, Kingdom International Alliance
San Diego

My friend, Pastor Rae Orozco, has provided an excellent and anointed work on healing the racial divide in *He Had to Go There*. I commend this work to you, and my prayer is that God will convict your heart as He has mine to be an instrument of healing and reconciliation. We must not be silent or inactive any longer. Jesus demonstrated and accomplished the work of reconciliation. That is why only the Gospel of Jesus Christ is God's solution to our divisions, our prejudices, and our sin.

I encourage you to partner with us and "go there!"

—Dr. Teresa Holder
State Women's Director
Church of God, DelMarVa D.C.

In her new book, Dr. Rae Orozco lays out a compelling call for Christian leaders to reexamine how we view those we are called to reach with the Gospel. Mixing both relevant Biblical insights and years of strategic cross-cultural ministry experience, she helps us confront the ugly roots of prejudice that lurk within the church and hinders the advance of the Gospel both at home and around the world. Dr. Orozco also lays out an inspiring and doable blueprint for truly loving, reaching, and serving people—regardless of ethnicity, gender, or cultural diversity—the way Jesus did. We must cross the cultural divides because Jesus has already led the way there.

—Dr. Richard Casteel
FMI Emissary to Central America and Spiritual Life Coach
International Church of the Foursquare Gospel

I can't even begin to say how helpful this book is. There is so much power and information from beginning to end. Pastor Rae is "on point" as she navigates a critical and much-needed discussion for Kingdom citizens—*He Had to Go There*.
This is a must-read for all.

—Bishop Doyle P. Scott Sr.
Director of Intercultural Advancement Ministries
Church of God International

If you are a true follower of Jesus Christ, you must follow His example and exemplify His life in yours. In her new book, Pastor Rae Orozco has made that mandate clear. If we are of Christ, we too must "go there." We are one race, and it is past time that the church of Jesus Christ model that truth.
There is not a separate Christianity for each ethnicity on earth. The Cross satisfied God's wrath once and for all, for everyone. He poured His wrath out on His only begotten Son.
For reconciliation to be horizontal, it must first be vertical. If we do not get Christ right, we will never treat each other right. The remedy for disunity, injustice, and division is anchored in Jesus Christ.

—Bishop Stan Holder
State Administrative Bishop
Church of God, DelMarVa D.C.

I want to express my sincere gratitude to Pastor Rae Orozco for the prayer, time, and hard work that went into writing this much-needed book. It is in the spirit of love that Pastor Rae uses truth to open our eyes to the need for forgiveness, reconciliation, and hope for all who desire to love our neighbors as Christ commands. We know prejudice and racism are nothing new, for even the Apostle Peter struggled with his own bias, confessed his sin, and crossed the racial divide of his day.

There is much I could write regarding my very negative experiences in and outside of the church as an African-American female preacher, yet I feel the call has been placed upon my sister, colleague, and spiritual daughter to take up this task in this hour. She has her own personal experiences to share that I believe will open eyes and soften hearts.

We cannot expect the victims of racism and prejudice to bear the responsibility to bring about change. We must all take responsibility for communicating that only healing, not hatred, can close the racial divide.

My prayer is that all of us will intentionally "go there" and be instrumental in bringing an end to the great hurt that many amongst us have experienced over the years. Start wherever you are and *go there* so our Lord will be glorified, the church will be edified, and the sinner will be evangelized.

—Evangelist Jacqueline Smith
National Evangelist, Church of God International

Pastor Rae Casteel is a voice with relevancy and revelation of Scripture for this generation. She is rooted in the absolute truth of God's Word and is authentic in her walk with Christ. Her passion and commitment to go "there" to bring people of all backgrounds and introduce them to her Savior is compelling to everyone God brings across her path. This book challenges us to continue in our missional mandate of making His Church a place for all ages, all races, and all social classes. We must engage in the "uncomfortable, difficult, and often messy" assignment of a bold, multiethnic church!

—Bishop Shea Hughes

State Administrative Bishop
Church of God, Arizona

Unless otherwise noted, Scripture quotations are taken from *The Holy Bible, New International Version®*. NIV®. Copyright © 1973, 1978, 1984, 2011 by International Bible Society. Used by permission of Zondervan Publishing House. All rights reserved.

Scripture quotations marked KJV are from the King James Version of the Holy Bible.

Scripture quotations marked NKJV are taken from the *New King James Version*. Copyright © 1979, 1980, 1982, 1990, 1995, Thomas Nelson, Inc., Publishers.

Scripture quotations marked NLT are taken from the *Holy Bible, New Living Translation*, copyright © 1996, 2004, 2007, 2012. Used by permission of Tyndale House Publishers, Inc., Wheaton, Illinois 60189. All rights reserved.

Director of Publications: David W. Ray
Managing Editor of Publications: Lance Colkmire
Editorial Assistant: Elaine McDavid
Graphic and Layout Design: Michael McDonald

ISBN: 978-1-64288-218-6

Copyright © 2022 by Pathway Press

All rights reserved. No part of this publication may be reproduced or transmitted in any form or by any means, electronic or mechanical, including photocopying, recording, or otherwise, or by any information storage or retrieval system, without the permission in writing from the publisher.

Please direct inquiries to Pathway Press, 1080 Montgomery Avenue, Cleveland, TN 37311. *www.pathwaypress.org*

DEDICATION

To my dear home-grown and faith-grown sons and daughters who embody the color and diversity of this world and whose identities are found in the grace and culture of the Kingdom. Pastors Adina and Trevor Kring; Pastor Saby Andino; Pastor Safari and Eto Kalunga; Danny and Ruby Lopez; Matthew and Justine Stone; Lindsay Houck; Pierce, Ester, and Giovana Orozco—you have enriched my life beyond words. This book is dedicated to you because you model multicultural ministry values, displaying courage, character, and capacity that constantly inspires me. May you always boldly and passionately "go there" for Christ!

ACKNOWLEDGEMENTS

Dr. Fidencio Burgueno: Like Barnabus did for Saul, you dared to pick me up, dust me off, and become a father to me personally and ministerially. Your gentleness, wisdom, and steadfast encouragement have nurtured and emboldened my spirit, enriched my life, and guided my steps. *Gracias Papi, soy tu hija.*

Pastor Adina Kring: As salt goes with pepper, coffee with cream, and ebony with ivory, we were supernaturally coupled as friends and ministry partners. My greatest Jesus adventures have happened with you by my side, as we've prayed, preached, wept, and laughed together. Thank you, my friend, for midwifing this book until its birth. You will always be my BFF.

Bishop Mitchell Corder: As a mentor and motivator, you impart an invaluable resource of assessable wisdom and prophetic discernment in every conversation. I am eternally grateful for your generosity in counsel, insight, and support.

Prophetess Jacquie Smith: Because you went there, I could go there. Every person of color and woman in ministry within our denomination salutes you for your unwavering courage, steadfast character, and unshakable faith. Thank you, Mother Jacquie, for leaving a bold heeled footprint so we can follow.

Tammy Rockwell: Sharp-witted and honest, many may not see the deep wellspring of compassion, generosity, and selflessness that resides within your heart. Thank you for giving hundreds of hours in research and editing so this project could reach the hands and hearts of nations. I am proud you are my friend.

Many thanks as well to Dr. Tim Hill, Dr. Raymond Culpepper, David Ray, Lance Colkmire, Sister Dorothy Sibley, Dr. Bill Lee, Reverend Doyle Scott, Pastor Travis Hall, Dr. Fijoy Johnson, Pastor Sandra Kay Williams, Yvette Santana, Pastors Trevor and Adina Kring, Pastor Safari Kalunga, Pastor Saby Andino, Matthew and Justine Stone who supported, advised, emboldened, and encouraged the writing of this book.

CONTENTS

Preface 19
Forewords 21

I. THE MANDATE 27
1 He Went There 29
2 Let's Go There 43
3 There It Is 51

II. THE MOTIVATION 71
4 What's Love Got to Do With It? 73
5 Going Back for the Future 87
6 Let's Kill This Giant 101
7 Prayers of a Dying Man 123

III. THE MISSION 143
8 'We' Starts With 'Me' 145
9 Forward Vision 169
10 From Ambivalence to Ambassadors 185

IV. THE MINISTRY 205
11 Bricks and Mortar 207
12 Nuts and Bolts 229
   The Final Challenge 243
   Recommended Resources 245

PREFACE

Jesus had to go *there,* John 4:4 tells us. Christ marched His bewildered disciples to the ancient well outside the town of Sychar in Samaria, not because it was a geographic necessity, but instead, a spiritual urgency. There Jesus would reach out to the disdained, deceived, and disregarded Samaritan people and include them in His love embrace. In doing so, He would also bring a holy confrontation with His disciple's smug ideological, theological, and cultural contempt for these marginalized people. This clash between earthly and Kingdom cultures would vividly confront long-held rationalized sins of racism and sexism.

There is a rising, clarion call of the Holy Spirit today that we, His Church, intentionally and purposefully *go there too.* For racial and cultural diversity, has been Christ's vision since He dragged His dumbfounded disciples to Jacob's well in the heat of the noonday sun. We were given a multicultural mandate. The insistence and persistence of our Lord's Great Commission to *go there* increases in its urgency as the Last Days draw closer. We cannot effectively answer the call to make disciples of all nations if we remain racially segregated and divided. By personally and corporately recognizing and repenting of the devilish deception of prejudice within the history, doctrines, and practices of the Church, we will start a holy revolution leading to reconciliation, unity, and multicultural partnership. If we will muster our courage to follow Christ's commanding footsteps *there,* we will see the beauty, synergy, and effectiveness of racial diversity in ministry. In the churches I've been honored to lead, I've discovered the purpose and power of multicultural ministry in both its messiness and its marvelous miracle. This is written to inspire through the example and mandate of Scripture, the inspiration and courage of our forerunners, and the personal experiences of my own life and ministry, that we must be courageous and without hesitation, "Go there."

FOREWORDS

After the brutal murder of George Floyd at the hands of a Minnesota police officer, the nation was thrown into a season of racial and political strife. Systemic racism was at the forefront of heated debates on police and law enforcement reform, along with enduring socioeconomic disparities in Black communities, and the church's history regarding racism was placed under the microscope. This intense examination revealed that the body of Christ for too long had been complacent or even complicit in its acceptance of racism and race supremacy. It was at the height of all of this that an international news network opened its broadcast stating, *"This is a moment of reckoning on race for the Christian church."*

This news reporter was expressing what many insightful and now frustrated prophetic minds and voices within the body of Christ felt and expressed for many decades, which is the need to address racism and discrimination within the church and its need to rid itself of this sinful cancer. A cancer that threatens to split Christ's body into many pieces and remove our ability to be an example to a dying world. In the words of Dr. Tony Evans, an African-American and senior pastor of Oak Cliff Bible Fellowship in Dallas, Texas: *"We cannot expect to solve the racial problem in our nation if we do not, and have not, even begun to solve it in the church."*

What has been even more frustrating and bewildering is the fact that racism became both the acceptable sin of the church and that unaddressable issue that few would dare to confront. In other words, the God-ordained leaders throughout the Kingdom simply responded like they did not want to go there. It is for this reason that I am grateful for the boldness, the heart of love, and the prophetic voice of Pastor Rae Orozco who, in the words of the title of her book, has dared to go there. This tremendous woman of God has undoubtedly been prepared, anointed, and raised up for such a time as this. She has been greatly used by God to be a trailblazer and God-ordained voice to speak to the issues of racism, unity, reconciliation, and gender equality in the state of Arizona and throughout the nation. Her experience as a pastor of a multicultural and multilingual church in Arizona has prepared her with a heart of compassion and a great understanding of the complexities and difficulties involved when God requires us to confront citizens of the Kingdom regarding this sensitive subject.

In this book, Pastor Rae thoroughly deals with the need for reconciliation from a historical, Biblical, and experiential level, and calls on the body of Christ to unify and take the lead as God intends for us to do. As a friend and colleague of Pastor Rae who serves in the same denomination, I am grateful for her tremendous impact within the Church of God and the Christ-like example she has continued to display as she has faced the many challenges that are common to a woman God has called to blaze such a trail. I am grateful for her sacrifice and stand as she continues to carve out a path for those who shall benefit from her work in the days to come.

For all who have a heart for multicultural ministry . . . for all who long for racial and ethnic reconciliation and unity . . . for all who desire to see the body of Christ become what Christ desires it to become . . . I strongly recommend this outstanding book written from the heart of an amazing woman of God. Thank you, Pastor Rae Orozco, for allowing the Lord to use you to bless the kingdom of God with this outstanding book.

—William A. Lee II
Lead pastor, Victorious Life Church
Conyers, Georgia

In the United States, we are seeing events take place that are shaking the foundations of our nation, such as political turmoil, social injustice, and division between the racial and ethnic groups.

In the middle of all the chaos, the church has within its grasp the greatest instruction manual known to humankind—the Bible. Yet, what is the benefit of having the greatest book ever written with the grand plan for humankind if we do not actively implement that plan? The church is called to represent the kingdom of God in all its diversity. It is called to unity and equity, but unfortunately, the church in the United States has not fully reflected that Kingdom mandate. In fact, although God's Word emphasizes we are all equal in His sight, our nation has excused racism, bias, and prejudice. The church has at times been sometimes complicit and too often complacent.

The saying goes, "Preacher, your actions speak so loud I cannot hear what you are saying." This upcoming generation has become cynical regarding the things of God because the church has been hypocritical regarding racial issues. We can no longer value patience and process over justice and equality.

In this season, God is raising up voices that not only speak out but also authentically model a Biblical principle and mandate. Pastor Rae Orozco is one of those individuals who embodies the essence of the message of oneness and multicultural ministry. I have been a mentor and spiritual father to Pastor Rae during her pastoral journey and have seen God use her to build multicultural ministries that extend to the nations and unite diverse people. This book, *He Had To Go There: The Multicultural Mandate,* establishes a Biblical principle, imparts Christ's passion for diversity, and offers practical tools that leaders may implement within their organizations. This is a "for such a time as this" book from a woman who is being raised up like Esther for these last days.

—Dr. Fidencio Burgueño
Regional Administrative Bishop
Church of God South Central Hispanic Region

When the Church of God was birthed in a rural North Carolina meetinghouse in 1886, the small band of nine believers were together in prayer and agreement for a movement committed to the New Testament, which admonishes Christ's followers to "go into *all the world* and preach the gospel to *all creation*" (Mark 16:15). In what would later be renamed the Church of God, the Christian Union embraced outreaches as it slowly expanded into the surrounding communities in the southeast United States, which included people groups such as Native American Cherokees.

Throughout its history, the Church of God has recognized the Scriptural mandate of inclusivity of all races, colors, and creeds. Rebecca Barr, an African-American woman and her husband, Edmond, a native Bahamian, set off on a ship in 1910 to evangelize in the Bahama Islands. The two became the first missionaries to venture outside the borders of the U.S. for the Church of God.

While the term *multicultural* did not become mainstream until the 1930s, the Church of God has been a multicultural church ever since the Barrs' pioneer voyage. It marked the beginning of more than a century of Pentecostal witness around the globe, now reaching into 185 countries on six continents.

It has been my honor to serve the Church of God in the capacities of director of World Missions and as general overseer. Within these roles, I have been privileged to observe the multicultural ministry and diversity within our church. Yet, as Pastor Orozco astutely points out in this book, there are challenges among all movements to become a truly New Testament church that reflects the cultural diversity that began in Acts 10, when Peter said, "I now realize how true it is that God does not show favoritism but accepts from *every nation* the one who fears Him and does what is right." (Acts 10:34-35).

The Church of God has a history of being intentional through the adoption of General Assembly resolutions and proclamations related to racial and ethnic diversity, as well as multiculturalism. We have implemented multicultural and ethnic programs with proactivity. In my ministry journey, I have strived to make multicultural ministry a part of my leadership emphasis, stressing that people of all colors, ethnicities, cultures, and tribes make up the family of God.

In the General Assembly address following my installation as general overseer in 2016, I announced the FINISH Commitment— a global church focus on the Great Commission. I am grateful that our church has embraced this acronym, which is infused with multicultural mandates: **FIND** the unreached people groups around the world; **INTERCEDE** in prayer; **NETWORK** servant leaders of all generations; **INVEST** our resources through strategic partnerships; **SEND** disciples to all nations; and reap a world of **HARVEST** with a global church focus.

Pastor Rae's primary desire in this work is "that we will all be encouraged to embrace the Biblical mandate for multicultural ministry, as well as have tools to implement ethnic diversity in our own churches and ministries." You will read in the final chapter her statement that "until we collectively and collaboratively present an authentic and credible witness of Christ's body, in all its diversity, we will not be able to effectually finish our Great Commission." This, too, is my heart's desire for the Church of God.

—Dr. Timothy M. Hill
General Overseer, Church of God International
Cleveland, Tennessee

I. THE MANDATE

An official order or commission to do something; the authority to carry out a policy or course of action.

1

He Went There

He *had* to go there. Jesus just had to go *there*. "He had to go through Samaria," John 4:4 (NLT) says. His disciples were bewildered as to why, for everyone knew good Jews would walk miles to not cross the Samaritan border: Faithful feet wouldn't step on Samaritan soil or holy hands touch Samaritan belongings; consecrated clothing wouldn't brush against Samaritan garments; and pious lips wouldn't drink from Samaritan vessels. A good Jew would never intentionally go near the miserable, half-breed, lawless, and doctrinally messed-up Samaritans. Except Jesus! He had to go *there*! Dragging His horrified disciples with Him, Jesus went to a town in Samaria called Sychar to meet a sinful woman at a well.

> When a Samaritan woman came to draw water, Jesus said to her, "Will you give me a drink?" (His disciples had gone into the town to buy food.) The Samaritan woman said to him, "You are a Jew and I am a Samaritan woman. How can you ask me for a drink?" (For Jews do not associate with Samaritans.) Jesus answered her, "If you knew the gift of God and who it is that asks you for a drink, you would have asked him and he would have given you living water" (John 4:7-10).

In a simple short conversation, weighted in historical and spiritual significance, Jesus transformed a lonely woman's heart, embraced an ostracized community, and instigated a multicultural Gospel revolution. He intentionally chose the setting: a contested well with a despised people group. Many accounts in the Bible include Samaritans. In the Gospels, Jesus featured the hatred between the Jews and the Samaritans in several of His parables. To understand the animosity, we need a basic awareness of its history.

In 721 B.C., the northern kingdom of Israel was conquered by the Assyrians. Most of the Jews were captured and taken forcibly to Assyrian lands as slaves. A small number were left in Israel to intermarry with Assyrian colonists and rebuild the cities after the invasion. The Jews who remained absorbed Assyrian traditions and religious practices, creating a hybrid culture and heretical worship. These people became known as the Samaritans.

When Nehemiah led the campaign to rebuild the walls of Jerusalem, the Samaritans aggressively opposed him, as recorded in Nehemiah 6:1-14. This event incited an enduring and seething hatred between Jews and Samaritans. The two cultures, though brothers by blood, moved further apart. Contempt for each other fomented so greatly, the Jews despised Samaritans even more than they hated Gentiles. Though the Jews regarded the Samaritans as ignorant, superstitious, and beyond God's grace, the Samaritans were still part of God's plan and well within His merciful reach.[1] So, Jesus purposefully crossed that physical Samaritan border—not because of geographic necessity, but by the divine imperative of the Holy Spirit—to go to a people who had suffered from deception, racism, and discount for hundreds of years. He had to go *there*!

THEY WENT THERE

Our spiritual predecessors dared to follow Jesus' example and went "there" too. The history of the church is rich in mission and mandate. A legacy written in the blood, sweat, and tears of those who refused to allow the vast possibilities of God to be unrealized by the confines of natural, ethnic, or spiritual boundaries. They had dreams, accompanied by determination, which fueled their fearless journeys across uncharted terrain.

In Acts 10 we read how the Apostle Peter risked being shunned to step across the threshold of a Roman Gentile's home. Likewise, the Apostle Paul chose paucity over privilege and set sail as an emissary for Christ to the foreign soil of the Gentile world. Compelled by Christ's command to "go" (Matthew 28:19), the disciples of the early church trudged through valleys, scaled mountains, sailed oceans, weathered hardship, braved poverty, endured persecution, and taunted death. All this, so those from other lands, languages, and cultures could know the love of Jesus.

WORLD-SHAKERS AND CULTURE-MAKERS

The halls of time echo with the songs, sermons, and supplications of those who dared to step out on liquid faith to follow Jesus "there." Imperfect vessels, these men and women are not honored here because of flawless lives or untainted liturgy. Instead, they are esteemed for the heavenly revelation that inspired gritty determination and sacrifice. Fearless and selfless, they spurned every intimidation to forge a passageway for the Gospel. These are a few of my heroes:

Patrick of Ireland was the real person behind the holiday and a remarkable individual despite religious legend. He was born many years before the Reformation, sometime between 224 to 415 A.D., to a Roman nobleman. Patricius, otherwise known to us as "Saint Patrick," grew up in a privileged life with servants and significant wealth. When Patrick was sixteen years old, he was captured by raiders, pirated to Ireland, and sold as a slave to a ferocious Celtic king. Despite being treated cruelly for years, Patrick had a life-changing encounter with Christ that transformed his heart and illuminated his purpose.

After several miserable years of servitude, Patrick escaped his captors, returned to his homeland, and dedicated himself to the study of Christianity, becoming a church bishop. As he served, Patrick's heart turned back to those who had previously oppressed him. In a vision, he saw the people of Ireland crying out, "We beg you . . . to come and walk among us." Without hesitation, he returned to Ireland to preach the Gospel. Utilizing what he learned in his former captivity, Patrick confronted oppressive and brutal Celtic paganism and won hearts with Christ's patience and compassion. "And we know that through him, the Gospel reached Ireland in a counter-cultural way—not by imperial force or an empire's expansion, but by his patient efforts to win the Irish to Christ in humility and peace."[2] *He went there.*

Father Eusebio Francisco Kino, a 17th-century Jesuit priest, traveled from Italy to bring a message of peace to the people of the Sonoran Desert. With a focus on the love and justice of God through Jesus Christ, Father Kino left a legacy as an advocate and bridge-builder between the various cultures and tribes living in the Mexican/American borderlands. He preached a simple and inclusive message, fighting vehemently against the forced labor of the native indigenous people in the silver mines and standing against the established religious and governmental oppression of Indigenous tribes. The San Xavier mission, built by those impacted by Father Kino's faith, still rises like a white dove out of the dusty desert landscape as a testament to the influence of one who *went there.*

John Wesley lived during the beginning of the 18th century, when England was in a spiritual bog, sinking rapidly into deep moral sludge. The organized national church had an undefined, vague message that brought little hope or light to the soul of the nation. As a young minister, Wesley experienced a profound and transformational encounter with the person and power of Jesus. He picked up the revival torch and stepped onto the platform of purpose. Not welcomed in most of the Church of England churches and frowned on as a fanatic, he went, like Jesus, to the "highways and byways" (Luke 14:23): to the poor in prisons, hospitals, workhouses, and the mine pit. *Wesley went there.*

The revival Wesley sparked moved across denominational lines and touched every class of society. He spoke out strongly against the slave trade and encouraged its abolition. England was transformed. So much so, in 1928 Archbishop Davidson wrote, "Wesley practically changed the outlook and even the character of the English nation."[3]

The Asian Bible Women of the 1800s and early 1900s were women who, despite the low position of females in Asian society, flooded their countries with the message of the power of Christ's love and salvation. *They went there,* facing poverty, persecution, and even death. They not only learned to read and write but also studied Christian doctrine and medicine. These hardy women brought healing to both soul and body to thousands of Asian people. Among those most renowned was a lady named Dora Yu, who crossed over the border of China to Korea in 1897 to preach the Gospel. Returning to her native land of China years later, she led the young Watchman Nee and his mother, Peace Lin, to Christ at a revival meeting. Watchman Nee became a most notable and effective evangelist and author to his generation.[4]

Amanda Berry Smith was born as a slave in Long Green, Maryland on January 23, 1837. A self-educated washerwoman, she became a gifted preacher and missionary. Preaching to thousands of souls regardless of color or context, she illustrated God's Word with engaging sermons and demonstrations of God's power. During a forty-five-year ministerial career, she preached on four continents, enduring intense opposition to women in public ministry, white racist violence, and the clenched fist of segregation. In her later days, she wrote books, opened orphanages, and became a highly respected faith leader and inspiration to men and women around the world. Oh, didn't *she just go there!*[5]

William Joseph Seymour, born to former slaves in Louisiana, was so shy he would stoop behind a wooden crate as he ministered on Azusa Street in 1906. His humble demeanor and undauntable courage positioned him to be one of the primary catalysts of the Pentecostal Movement. From the birth of the revival in Los Angeles, he *went there*, rejecting all racial barriers and any hindrance to women in church leadership. Welcome in the revival meetings were people of all ethnicities: Blacks, Latinos, and Whites who side-by-side received the baptism in the Holy Spirit and spoke in new tongues.[6] So powerful was Pastor Seymour's ministry, it compelled a white Southerner, G. B. Cashwell from the Church of God in Cleveland, Tennessee, to traverse across the country so this one-eyed black man would lay hands on him to receive a greater impartation of the baptism in the Holy Spirit.[7]

Aimee Semple McPherson, a Canadian-born farm girl, traveled in her "gospel car" in the early and mid-1900s, holding tent revivals and healing rallies across the United States. Her animated style of preaching—which included illustrated sermons, costumes, actors, and imaginative backdrops—filled tents, auditoriums, and halls with people eager to hear and see a living-color presentation of the Gospel. The healing power that flowed from her left abandoned crutches, wheelchairs, and gurneys at the altars, and empty ambulances in the parking lot. Refusing the pressure to bar admittance to people of color to her meetings, she boldly stood her ground and welcomed all, winning her the title, "Everybody's Sister." Undaunted by sexism, racism, or scandal, *she went there,* positioning her famously heeled foot upon uncharted territory: buying a radio station, building the famous domed Angeles Temple with cash, feeding more people daily during the Great Depression than the government, and founding the International Foursquare Church denomination.[8]

Maria Atkinson, a young Mexican wife and mother, while sick with cancer, heard from her maid of the healing power of Jesus Christ. Filled with faith, Maria prayed this simple prayer: "Lord, if You will complete my healing so that none can doubt it and give me this experience of the Holy Spirit baptism, I'll take this message to Mexico, to my family." She was immediately healed and filled with the Holy Spirit, then set straightway to preach the Gospel and open new churches. Many from all denominations came to hear her regardless of class distinctions. Signs, wonders, and healings consistently followed Maria's ministry. God sovereignly protected her from government attacks and religious persecution.

Though unrecognized as an apostolic leader by her denomination, Maria was never ruffled by the voices of mere men, choosing to answer instead to the bass resonance of God's captivating call. She expanded her ministerial territory to open Bible schools across Mexico, training hundreds of pastors and missionaries. Her dynamic ministry spread throughout her homeland and even into the United States, making her one of the primary founders of the Full Gospel Church of God in Latin America. Her life is a potent testimony of *one who went there* in the power and passion of Christ. On her tombstone is written her life message, "Here there are no doubts."[9]

Dr. Martin Luther King was perhaps the most impactful civil-rights leader of our time. In less than 13 years of ministry and leadership, Dr. King achieved more progress toward racial equality in America than had occurred in the previous 350 years. A pastor, minister, and skilled orator, his Biblically inspired passion for equality led him to step onto the stage of history. Advocating for the power of words and acts of nonviolent resistance, he led protests, marches, demonstrations, and campaigns, mobilizing and emboldening people of every color to stand against overt and systemic racism and poverty. His personal march for justice ended tragically and abruptly on April 4, 1968 in Memphis, Tennessee. Yet his compelling and forceful words continue to inspire, illuminate, and motivate the generations that we should also *go there.*[10]

If these pages could contain it, we would chronicle the accounts of countless other Christian world-shakers and culture-makers, such as Martin Luther, George Muller, John Carey, George Whitefield, Richard Allen, Sojourner Truth, Hudson Taylor, Watchman Nee, Jareena Lee, William and Evangeline Booth, Jim Elliot, Corrie Ten Boom, Mother Theresa, Cameron Townsend, Billy Graham, and so many more. Some names are well known to us, their exploits rehearsed and revered; some are unfamiliar to us, yet well-known to Heaven. Holding to differing church backgrounds and liturgical practices, they were yet uniform and unified in uncompromising faith in Christ and unquenchable passion for people.

He Went There

From the church's infancy, spiritual heroes from every generation, denomination, tongue, and color have broken down barriers, crossed borders, and challenged stereotypes to reach further with the Gospel. They are our forerunners, who broke ground and lit the way so the next generations of border crossing pioneers could pick up the torch and *go there* too. The writer of Hebrews accurately proclaimed in 11:16, "Therefore God is not ashamed to be called their God"; and in verse 38, "The world was not worthy of them."

A story not known to many, but a priceless treasure to me, is my own family's faith legacy. My grandparents, both maternal and paternal, began their missionary adventures in the mid-1950s in Cuba just before the Castro revolution. Forsaking all their belongings and the comforts of friends, family, and the familiar, they went boldly, unacquainted with Cuban culture or the Spanish language. With hearts affirmed in the call of God and aflame with evangelistic zeal, they each crossed their own borders: one grandfather left his California farmlands and the other, the Canadian timberlands. My grandparents worked there, pressed past personal lack and persecution, to foster generation-spanning relationships and transformed lives. When the population wearied of the corruption in the Batista government, the ruthless communist philosophy of Castro took hold of the country, and the spiritual climate shifted dramatically.

Late one evening, as my family's missionary caravan traveled home from an evangelistic meeting, Castro rebels attacked their jeeps, mistaking them for Batista soldiers. The barrage of shooting exploded on the night's quiet ride, causing shrieks of agony from the driver, who was shot through the windshield into his eye and forehead. My mother, a teenager at the time, also screamed as thumb-sized bullets shattered her heel and pulverized her ankle and calf muscles. My grandfather immediately leaped from the jeep to halt the assault, and then began to share the Gospel. Minutes later those same fierce soldiers laid down their weapons and bent their knees to receive the grace and forgiveness of Jesus. Former assailants became armed escorts for the bullet-ridden caravan, as it wound its way slowly over rough dirt roads to a hospital in a city nearby.

Miraculously, the driver survived, though he lost his right eye in the fray. My mother, after a long convalescence, walked again, not only on Cuban soil but upon many other foreign lands. To this day, she bears the scars of a shattered heel and bullet fragments in her legs—a testament to the miracle and the moment of her Holy Spirit infilling and personal ministry call. Despite this horrific attack, my grandparents continued to minister with unflinching faith in Cuba until the Castro government confiscated their homes and churches and evicted them from the country. After being expelled from Cuba, my mother's parents ministered in southern Mexico, Mozambique, and Portugal. Meanwhile, my paternal grandparents made a small boat their home and sailed the Caribbean, preaching in the various islands. A few years later, they and my newlywed parents accepted an invitation to minister together in northern Mexico.

Into this missionary landscape, I was born. My earliest childhood memories are of voices lifted in worship in the Spanish language, of earthen church floors in humble wooden buildings, built by hand by my grandfather and father in the hot Sinaloa sun. I can still envision my small white hand clasped happily in my friend's brown hand, raised together in friendship, prayer, and praise. This is my heritage—because my grandparents *went there*.

OUR TURN

What would the church be today if its patriarchs through the generations had not been willing to *go there* at all cost? The great majority of us would have never even heard of the name of Jesus! Thank God for their undiluted courage, selfless sacrifice, patient perseverance, and tireless tenacity. Yet the legacy they've left us demands much more than merely grateful hearts. We are compelled by them and the Holy Spirit to go there too: to move beyond our cultural comfort zones and follow their fiery footsteps across the borderlines of racial, gender, and cultural barriers. Hebrews 12:1-2 allows us to peer into the heavenlies to see the eager faces of our heroic predecessors, leaning forward in anticipation of our response:

> Therefore, since we are surrounded by such a great cloud of witnesses, let us throw off everything that hinders and the sin that so easily entangles. And let us run with perseverance the race marked out for us, fixing our eyes on Jesus, the pioneer, and perfecter of faith. For the joy set before him, he endured the cross, scorning its shame, and sat down at the right hand of the throne of God.

If there ever was a time to go there, it is now. Violence fills homes, streets, and boils among the nations. Racism is rampant, systemic, and "justified" not only in the United States, but throughout the world, and sadly solidified even in the church. Politics divide our nation, alienating even Christians from one another. The younger generation is disillusioned and cynical. Our world is desperate and hopeless. Some weep for past heroes: the voice of one like Martin Luther King Jr. and the courage of a Corrie Ten Boom. Yet, God did not choose these honored saints to walk in these last days. No, instead, He purposed, placed, and positioned you and me to live and lead in this day; fashioning and forming us specifically for these times. Mordecai's famous words to Esther reverberate especially now: we have been "called for such a time as this" (Esther 4:14). Therefore, let us say "yes" to God's clarion call! Let us bravely place our feet upon the path of purpose, and with unswerving determination, *go there*!

Endnotes

1. https://margmowczko.com/a-brief-history-of-the-samaritans
2. Kaylena Radcliff, *Torchlighters: Heroes of Faith* (www.Torchlighters.org)
3. www.christianity.com/church/church-history/timeline/1701-1800/evangelical-revival-in-england
4. Cindy Jacobs, *Women of Destiny* (Gospel Light, 1998)
5. Jacobs, *Women of Destiny*
6. Dale T. Irvin, "Drawing All Together In One Bond of Love" (www.revival-library.org)
7. Chris Green, "The Spirit That Makes Us (Number) One: Racism, Tongues, and the Evidences of Spirit Baptism" (Southeastern University)
8. Foursquare.org/ history/Everybody's Sister
9. www.cogwm.org/news/maria-atkinson-missionary-hero and Charles W. Conn, *Like a Mighty Army: The History of the Church of God* (Pathway Press, 2008)
10. thekingcenter.org/about-dr-king/

2

Let's Go There

I accepted the challenge to become lead pastor of a predominately white church in Tucson, Arizona, over 17 years ago. God gave my husband and me what some assumed was an impossible dream: a church filled with people of many colors, cultures, and backgrounds, united by Christ's grace and partnered together in missional purpose.

Many believed a multicultural and multilingual church in Arizona was a futile fantasy. The Southwest's history is steeped in racial and gender prejudice, independence, and violence, all the way back to the Spanish-Mexican wars and indigenous tribal conflicts. Despite a colorful weave of Latin and Native American heritage, rugged pioneer settlers, and Black Buffalo Soldiers, a deeply entrenched demonic principality of racial hostility has ruled for hundreds of years over the Sonoran Desert sand. Arizonans sometimes still exhibit a "Shoot now and let God sort it out later" mentality!

Yet, the message of inclusion and equality in Christ resonated, running counterculture to Arizona culture. The church grew rapidly in size and influence to include three congregations—English language, Spanish language, and African refugee. Each was diverse in color and background yet bonded together in doctrine and purpose.

Stepping into our "Unity Celebration" gatherings was to encounter a remarkable realm of color, texture, and sound. Joyous praise and dancing erupted in one aisle, while in the very next, reverent awe. Young people leaped in front, while aged white-haired matriarchs stood in the back like alabaster columns, arms lifted high. Whites, Blacks, Latinos, Asians, and Africans . . . architects and carpenters, doctors and housemaids . . . all worshiped side by side. There was liberty to express faith, culture, and uniqueness in an atmosphere of mutual respect and unified devotion to Jesus. United purpose created a convergence of gifting that produced community impact. Ministries developed and grew, giving access to otherwise closed-up people groups. Leaders were discipled, and the ministry advanced with new church plants and affiliations. Managing such a blend of people was sometimes chaotic, but most often, wonderfully divine.

It all seemed miraculous, and it was. Yet the miracle had a requirement. It required a willingness on our part to *go there* on a personal level: to move beyond cultural comfort zones and to initiate cross-cultural relationships. It took intentionality in expanding our cultural competency: to learn the strengths, values, and wounding of different people groups. It necessitated humility when inadvertently doing or saying ignorant and offensive things. We accepted that we would occasionally fail, but resolved to be courageous enough to ask forgiveness, learn, and try again.

THEREFORE, GO THERE

God was and continues to be divinely present in the amazing adventure. That is because a multicultural church is not only our dream; it is also Jesus' dream. In Matthew 28:19-20, Jesus said, "Go and make disciples of all the nations, baptizing them in the name of the Father and the Son and the Holy Spirit. Teach these new disciples to obey all the commands I have given you" (NLT).

Let's Go There

A multicultural, multiethnic church is not simply a missional mandate; it was a Pentecostal imperative. In Acts 1:8, Jesus said, "But you will receive power when the Holy Spirit comes upon you. And you will be my witnesses, telling people about me everywhere—in Jerusalem, throughout Judea, in Samaria, and to the ends of the earth" (NLT).

On the Day of Pentecost, fulfillment of the promise came: "And everyone present was filled with the Holy Spirit and began speaking in other languages, as the Holy Spirit gave them this ability" (2:4 NLT).

As the crowd gathered to see what was happening in verse 11, they exclaimed, "We all hear these people speaking in our own languages about the wonderful things God has done!" Acts 2:11 (NLT).

"At the Tower of Babel, language divided and dispersed people—spiritual language now brought them together," said Fidencio Burgueno, Church of God administrative bishop (July 12, 2015 sermon at Grace To the Nations). How true! Through the power of the Holy Spirit, people understood the message of the Gospel in their own cultural context. Spiritual language united them as one and expanded Kingdom culture. As the church was birthed on the Day of Pentecost, Peter stood to address the crowd:

> But this is that which was spoken by the prophet Joel;
> "And it shall come to pass in the last days, saith God, I will pour out of my Spirit upon all flesh: and your sons and your daughters shall prophesy, and your young men shall see visions, and your old men shall dream dreams: And on my servants and on my handmaidens, I will pour out in those days of my Spirit; and they shall prophesy" (Acts 2:16-18 KJV).

Pentecost was a day of prophetic fulfillment and miraculous inclusion! What was formerly reserved for a select group of male Jewish prophets, priests, and kings, was now lavishly poured out on men and women, young and old, of every nationality and language.

YES, "THERE"

However, looking at the history of the infant church as recorded in the Book of Acts, it's baffling that eight chapters later—even after Jesus' specific command to "tell people everywhere," and the infilling of the Holy Spirit at Pentecost—no one seemed willing to venture past Jerusalem or their Jewish cultural comfort zones. The Holy Spirit was insistent and incessant about *going there*. So, in Acts 10, Peter was confronted with the salvation and Holy Spirit baptism of a pork-eating Gentile named Cornelius. Finally, after this profound and persuading experience, Peter got it: he, too, had to go *there*.

Sadly, over two thousand years later, "the most segregated hour in this nation is Sunday at 11:00 am," as Dr. Martin Luther King Jr. observed. Across the world, but especially in the United States, Sunday remains the most racially divided day of the week. Believers cluster together in classes, races, and ages—working-class churches, affluent churches, young churches, senior churches, Black churches, White churches, Asian churches, and Latino churches. The divide is sadly much more than language barriers. We, like the Acts 2 believers, preach and minister to what we know and resemble. The U.S. church specifically, is, well . . . somewhat narcissistic. We are each comforted to see a similar image to our own reflected in the pews on Sundays. So, we gather according to our sameness, instead of obeying the missional mandate to "go to . . . all" (Matthew 28:19). Conveniently, we compartmentalize the

Great Commission to signify people groups across the oceans in other nations—certainly not people groups across town, or across the street. The result is congregations that look more like culture clubs, rather than Jesus' dream church.

Frankly, the American church today resembles the ethnic exclusivity found in the early church in the first nine chapters of Acts, not the boldly multiethnic church of Acts 10 and beyond. Perhaps that is because multicultural ministry is not an easy assignment. It can be uncomfortable, difficult, and often messy. Regardless, Jesus still *went there,* insisting the leaders and believers of the early church do so, too.

CHRIST IN LIVING COLOR

Pastor Mark DeYmaz, in his insightful book *Building a Healthy Multiethnic Church,* expounds how Acts 10 became the early church's pivot point. In summary, DeYmaz writes how after the Peter and Cornelius incident in Acts 10, church leaders finally became deliberate in crossing borders by sending Barnabas and Paul to the culturally and racially diverse city of Antioch (11:22-26).

As the message of Jesus' love reached the ears of the citizens of Antioch, a Gospel revolution began. Gentiles of every color, and from every part of the world—including Africa, Asia, and Europe—believed in and received Jesus. They became one regardless of race, language, or background, with leadership as distinct and diverse as had ever been seen prior (13:1-3). Acts 11:26 tells us it is here—in this multicultural, racially diverse group of people—the followers of Jesus "were first called Christians" (NLT). This is very significant. The word *Christian* means "like Christ" or "little Christ." We, the church, look most like Jesus not when we are segregated and separated—but when we as Whites,

Blacks, Asians, Latinos, and people of diverse ethnicities, worship and serve together. For it is together we become Christ in living color to the world. The Book of Acts reveals the church at Antioch had a great missional passion for the world and became the base for Gospel ventures to the Gentiles. Mark DeYmaz stated, "It was because the church at Antioch reflected the world that Jesus died for." In other words, they were passionate about the world because Christ was passionate about them.

KINGDOM COMPLEXION

From the start to its conclusion, Jesus' earthly ministry consistently sought out and gathered in those from other cultures, the young and the elderly, the poor and the rich, the healthy and the infirmed, the sinner and the Pharisee. Inclusivity and diversity were the trademarks of Christ's ministry. In Luke 4:18-19, He boldly declared His ministry mission was to cross over the boundaries of sin, prejudice, hopelessness, and oppression to bring salvation, dignity, and freedom:

> "The Spirit of the Lord is on me because he has anointed me to proclaim good news to the poor. He has sent me to proclaim freedom for the prisoners and recovery of sight for the blind, to set the oppressed free, to proclaim the year of the Lord's favor."

On every pathway, hillside, riverbank, and field; in every hut, house, courtyard, and synagogue, Jesus consistently extended His love and grace to those of every color, culture, background, and creed. He confounded the elite and delighted the lowly. He met a Pharisee in secret, called a thief out of a tree, and talked with a sinful Samaritan woman at a well. The mission was people—all people.

Even Christ's genealogy speaks of divine inclusion, listing foremothers Rahab (from Jericho in Cana) and Ruth the Moabite. His birth was heralded by an angelic choir to the lowliest in social ranking—the field shepherds, who were the first welcomed in His presence. His death broadcasted this same message. The official notice nailed above Him on the cross declared Jesus was the King of the Jews in the three most common languages of that day—Greek, Latin, and Hebrew, according to John 19:20. So, even as Christ died, Heaven was declaring,

> "Your blood has ransomed people for God from every tribe and language and people and nation. And you have caused them to become a Kingdom of priests for our God" (Revelation 5:9-10 NLT).

After the cross and just before His heavenly ascension, Christ's final words to His disciples focused primarily on the call to reach the "ethnos" or ethnicities of the world. In Matthew 28:19, Jesus commanded, "Go and make disciples of all the nations" (NLT), and in Acts 1:8, "You will be my witnesses, telling people about me everywhere—in Jerusalem, throughout Judea, in Samaria, and to the ends of the earth" (NLT).

The kingdom of God is very much about diversity and cultural inclusion. Ray Chang, president of the Asian American Christian Collaborative, said: "In the simplest of terms if you don't care about diversity, you don't care about the kingdom of God. Everything from the genealogy of Jesus to the vision in Revelation shouts diversity as a part of both the present and the eschatological vision of God's Kingdom." @tweetraychang

Jesus' dream church was multiethnic, multicultural, and intra-generational in its infancy, and it will be so in its fullest glory. We're given a snapshot of it in Revelation 7:9:

> After this I looked, and there before me was a great multitude that no one could count, from every nation, tribe, people, and language, standing before the throne and before the Lamb. They were wearing white robes and were holding palm branches in their hands.

Just a warning: If we don't like diversity in the church here on earth, we're going to hate Heaven. So, we might as well *go there now*!

3

There It Is

A wealthy senior woman booked a room at a posh New York hotel. She headed for her room and waited at the lobby elevator. When the elevator doors opened, two African American men were in the elevator, coming up from the basement parking. She hesitated, eyeing the tall men dressed in jeans and hoodies, and though still conflicted, she nervously stepped in and turned toward the closing elevator door. Obviously anxious, she fidgeted with her pearls and shifted her weight, feeling as though she would never arrive at her floor.

From behind her, a deep voice instructed in a whispered tone, "Lady, hit the floor." Horrified, she was paralyzed in fear. He spoke again, but more emphatically, "Lady, press the floor!" Now overcome by terror, she threw up her purse and hit the ground, sprawling on the elevator floor. There was momentary silence above her and then muffled giggles. Finally, the men said, "Lady, you need to press the button your floor is on!" They helped her back to her feet and she pressed the button to her floor, red-faced and gripping her purse in heated embarrassment as the elevator rose.

As soon as she exited the elevator, the men broke into hysterical laughter that echoed up the elevator shaft as they rose to the penthouse suite. Later that evening, a hotel bellman arrived at the woman's room holding several dozen roses. A tag attached read, "Madame, we are sorry you were frightened in the elevator, but thank you for the best laugh we'd had in a year!" Signed, Eddie Murphy and Michael Jordan.

NO LAUGHING MATTER

This funny story may or may not be true, but it helps to make the point: no matter who we are or where we come from, we all have a propensity for prejudice. It is an ugly yet innate human inclination to assume things about others who are not part of our people group. Almost unconsciously, we assess and evaluate people based on skin color, age, gender; how they talk, walk, sing, vote, smell, dress, tattoo, pierce; and even what they eat! We automatically categorize—we label and rank, separate and segregate.

All of us have heard comments that generalize and disparage people groups. Such things as, Asians are smart but drive really bad; Mexicans are lazy and probably "illegal"; the Irish drink and fight; and all Italians are in the mafia. (After all, haven't you watched *The Godfather*?) Maybe you've heard that Blacks are violent but can really sing, dance and jump; Whites are all racists; men are basically jerks; and women are too emotionally and spiritually fragile to lead.

We may not personally say these things out loud, and we may even giggle at how ridiculous they are when written here in black and white. Nonetheless, such notions become deeply embedded into our belief systems. In some cases, they materialize in overt and aggressive behavior and speech. More commonly these theories manifest in avoidance, silence, or acquiescence to race-based traditions. False pretenses are then furthered, misconceptions enabled, baseless fears fueled, and spiteful divisions perpetuated. Racism, sexism, and prejudice are the devil's most devious and effective weapons.

Jesus "had to go through Samaria." Oh, how I wish I could have been there when Jesus dragged his dumbfounded disciples to the town of Sychar! Behind Christ's steady and determined gait, His crew's puzzled expressions, raised eyebrows, and exasperated shrugs likely animated their march across the loathsome borderline. They undoubtedly tried to mask the smug ideological and cultural contempt they had for those soiled Samaritan sinners from their resolute leader. Jesus knew their hearts and had purposed His disciples for greater things. So, He intentionally navigated His course toward a Kingdom confrontation they would not forget. Jesus led them there—not only for the sake of the Samaritan woman, but also for the sake of His disciples. It was time to bring His pretentious and privileged followers face to face with their own Biblically rationalized sins of racism and sexism.

Recent events in the United States and around the world have compelled the church to recognize and reconcile its racist history and present systemic biases. We have been led to our own "there" by Jesus. That is because if we don't go there, we can't effectively go anywhere else. If we don't go there, we won't have the understanding or capacity to build racially diverse partnerships and multiethnic ministries in a world that is quickly becoming a global community.

THE S(K)IN ISSUE

So, here we go: Prejudging someone is simply prejudice. Prejudging someone because of their race is racism. More importantly, it is *sin*. "Racism is not simply a skin problem, but a sin problem," writes David A. Anderson.[1] In other words, it's not a skin issue, it's a *sin* issue. It is our sin-genetics that compel mankind to relabel others according to gender, skin tone, ability, and culture.

"It wasn't culture that caused the great divide among mankind—it was sin," says Trillia J. Newbell.[2] It is in our sin-DNA to rename and reframe others in a way that lessens their true God-given dignity and value. It came as an immediate result of sin entering the world in Genesis 3:12-21. Not only was mankind's relationship with God corrupted, but the unity and partnership between Adam and Eve also degenerated in blaming and domination (v. 20). Sin escalated in the next generation into jealousy and violence between their sons, Cain and Abel (4:1-9). So, it continued as humanity expanded: each clan, tribe, and people group identified itself differently, labeling the other group as inferior and fighting for preeminence.

Prejudice and racism are sins. It's time we stopped our excuses for these particular sins because of national or regional history, social ethos, or past wounding. We need to stop with the explanations, justifications, and alibis and just call it what it is—filthy, putrid, unholy, and utterly displeasing to our God.

ANIMATED DIRT

The heat in southern Arizona had been especially blistering one summer. When the monsoon storm clouds finally began to form, a collective sigh of relief was almost audible from its desert-dwelling inhabitants. As clouds burst and refreshing rain began to pour from the heavens, my two-year-old daughter and I ran out to the covered porch to enjoy the downpour together.

Just thirty minutes later, the furious storm dissipated, leaving the thirsty soil drenched, arroyos running like rivers, and the outside temperature finally livable. My little one—our third child and a late-in-life blessing—asked to play in the mud. My parenting style at this season of my life had devolved into more of a grandparenting permissiveness, so I waved her on to jump in the puddles and squish about in the muck. She ended up sitting in brown goo, gleefully squeezing and shaping a muddy masterpiece between her chubby fingers. When finished, she proudly held up two globs and declared, "Mommy and Daddy!"

The first man and woman were created in God's image and by God's own hands out of the dust of the ground. God gave them one name: *Adam,* the root meaning "red or ruddy as the earth."[3] Genesis 2:7 provides an unmistakable and intentional word-play:

> Then the Lord God formed a man [Adam] from the dust of the ground [Adamah] and breathed into his nostrils the breath of life, and the man became a living being (Genesis 2:7; inserts added).

Since the Hebrew word for earth is *Adamah,* God called mankind, "Adam" because we were drawn from the rich red dust of the ground. This means we are all just highly functioning dirt! We may be dirt from Africa, Asia, Mexico, or England, but we're still just dirt. Our only intrinsic value is that God breathed into us, making us living souls—dirt animated by His Holy Spirit. Discrimination occurs when one clump of clay assumes superiority over another clump of clay. It's quite absurd, but pride fuels the deception. As we know, pride in any form is a stench to God: "All of you, clothe yourselves with humility toward one another because, 'God opposes the proud but shows favor to the humble'" (1 Peter 5:5).

We cannot excuse, gloss over, or dress up masculine or feminine pride, racial pride, cultural pride, or even national pride as though it isn't somehow just plain ugly pride. As the old saying goes, putting lipstick on a pig doesn't mask the stench. For there is a significant difference between celebrating cultural heritage and distinctives and the repugnant sin of prejudice. One honors, incorporates, and builds up; the other denigrates, marginalizes, and belittles. Sadly, we as God's people have confused the two and excused the latter.

FROM HOLY TO PROFANE

The revival preacher, well-known in the faith community, was articulate, animated, and engaging. It was a great honor to be invited to minister with him at a ministers' conference in a prestigious Pentecostal church. Those in attendance had greatly anticipated our visit, resulting in services that were powerful and refreshing. After the final Sunday service, several ministers and church leaders gathered together for a meal of fellowship. I brought my oldest two young children along with me to the luncheon and introduced them proudly to my fellow guest speaker. He eyed them shrewdly, then looked up at me and said with a cynical laugh, "But those are N****** kids!" The room fell silent in shock. All eyes darted from the preacher to me, and then to the hosting leaders, curious at how we would respond.

Glancing down at my children, I saw my daughter wince and my son's eyes moisten. I had to fight my flesh hard not to jump over the table in my stiletto heels and give him a momma-bear lesson he'd not forget, in this "Oh no, you didn't" moment! Thankfully, the Holy Spirit caught and subdued me before the conference ended in the public arrest of its female speaker. Instead, I pushed my young children protectively behind me, looking for the host pastor or conference minister to respond. But they didn't. No one did. Only nervous laughter breached the stunned silence.

Realizing the leadership was going to let this comment pass, I met the preacher's eye and responded sternly: "How could you move between what is holy to the profane so easily? You just came off the pulpit where God used your lips to speak His Word. Now you're going to use that same tongue to denigrate my children because of their skin color?"

The preacher, unnerved by my intensity, stuttered his explanation: "I'm sorry. I was just making a joke."

Nope. Firmly, and without removing my gaze from him, I stated, "Sir, racism is not funny. It's sin."

"Well," he fidgeted, "you have to understand I was just brought up that way. I'm not racist—you saw me minister to everyone equally."

To my amazement, several in the room nodded their head in affirmation. Finding fuel from their silent approval, he leaned forward and challenged, "You're White. Don't you honor your own people, Pastor Rae?"

Too many Christian leaders still warm their cold hands at the heretical fire of prejudice, while it scorches the hearts and hopes of God's precious people of color. We may attempt to defend the lack of diversity in the pew as smart "marketing" to a specific demographic or ministry target group. We may even explain away an all-white board in a multiethnic organization as due to a complex bylaw matter. But we should check our hearts to ensure our ministry focus isn't just an expression of partiality to one group over another because of convenience, long-held traditions, economics, or just plain cultural elitism. Because God views exclusivity as contrary to the Gospel, which, through His grace, broke down every barrier between Himself and others. Paul wrote in Ephesians 2:13-19:

> But now in Christ Jesus you who once were far away have been brought near by the blood of Christ. For he himself is our peace, who has made the two groups one and has destroyed the barrier, the dividing wall of hostility, by setting aside in his flesh the law with its commands and regulations. His purpose was to create in himself one new humanity out of the two, thus making peace, and in one body to reconcile both to God through the cross, by which he put to death their hostility. He came and preached peace to you who were far away and peace to those who were near. For through him we both have access to the Father by one Spirit. Consequently, you are no longer foreigners and strangers, but fellow citizens with God's people and also members of his household.

CAUTION TAPE

My family moved into a house that required my two daughters to share a room. My oldest daughter, Ester, was in her early teens; my youngest, Gigi, was eight years her junior, and a very precocious preschooler. Both girls were excited about sharing their big room, planning the details of the décor and organization together. Boundaries of respect regarding personal space and property were agreed upon. Until one day we heard a riotous uproar coming from the girls' room. Ester was yelling and

Gigi was screeching. Fearful some horrible intruder had climbed through the window to harm our daughters, my husband and I dashed across the house. Instead, there was Gigi, her face painted brightly with Ester's new makeup, along with the floor, rug, walls, and bedspreads. Ester was furious.

My husband and I suppressed giggles as we comforted our distressed teenager and disciplined our preschooler. The importance of respect was reemphasized to both. But the next day, Gigi found it impossible to honor the invisible boundaries that kept her from her sister's belongings. This time, it was Ester's nail polish that covered the room. Ester's frustration boiled over, and Gigi's toys became the sad victims of Ester's rage. The situation continued for days despite our parental threats, bribes, and pleading. Our little Gigi had a strong sense of entitlement even the sternest discipline wasn't budging.

We had to do something for the sake of our family's peace and came up with a plan to separate the girls in a more visible way. Buying bright yellow "caution" tape, we strung it through the middle of the room, dividing the two girls' beds and belongings. The beautiful space became marred by the crude partition but created a visible boundary that helped the girls recognize one another's personal space. Gigi was to keep to her own side and never cross the yellow tape; Ester would do the same. So, finally, the two arrived at a passable way of living together. But they lost the joy and camaraderie of their sisterhood for a long time.

The church is segregated on Sunday morning for the same reasons my girls were. It is easier to divide and keep to our own rather than to work out our differences and show deference and inclusion. It's easier not to share the pew, the platform, the properties, and the boardroom. It is easier to keep things quiet and neat than to endure the messy business of making room for cultural uniqueness and ethnic expression in our services and ministries. It's easier—but it's not God, nor godly. We have traded the synergy and dynamic of brotherhood for uneasy and graceless family peace. The division has been necessary only because of our own spiritual immaturity. But it's time for the church to grow up and learn to share. It's time we take down the ugly caution tape of division that mars the beauty of God's house.

RADICAL REALIGNMENT

We recently bought a big old Ram truck for our teenage daughter. Taking it onto the freeway for the first time, I found myself constantly fighting the steering wheel from pulling to the right. Without a consistent course correction, it would surely veer off course and land us in a ditch. I was hesitant to fully press the accelerator and feel the power of the big engine until it visited the mechanic's shop. The mechanic said the truck needed realignment. The Apostle Paul did just that—a rough realignment—when openly confronting Peter for acquiescing to Jewish legalism and racism in Galatians 2:11-14:

> When Cephas [Peter] came to Antioch, I opposed him to his face, because he stood condemned. For before certain men came from James, he used to eat with the Gentiles. But when they arrived, he began to draw back and separate himself from the Gentiles because he was afraid of those who belonged to the circumcision group. The other Jews joined him in his hypocrisy, so that by their hypocrisy even Barnabas was led astray. . . . They were not acting in line with the truth of the gospel.

Even the Apostle Peter needed to be realigned. He had acquiesced to the Jewish Christians' bias by eating separately from the Gentiles when Christ had invited "the poor, the crippled, the blind and the lame" to His table (Luke 14:21). Paul made the point: There is no selective seating at Christ's table! Some may argue Galatians 2:11-14 is mainly about religious legalism. But to negate the underlying racial issues between the Jews and Gentiles is to ignore, not only Biblical history but also the four Gospels, where Jesus consistently provoked reactions from the Jews by including sinners, Samaritans, and Gentiles into His love-reach. The detailed account of the confrontation reveals even the early church, freshly infused with the generous Gospel, still had a propensity for prejudice. When it comes to race issues, church leaders must courageously and consistently redirect and realign the doctrines, practices, and systems of the church back to "the truth of the gospel" (v. 14).

UNMUZZLED

A good percentage of us, as Peter was, have been muzzled by intimidation. We may feel unskilled, unsure, and uneducated in addressing racial issues in a meaningful way. So, we have stayed silent when we should have been speaking. However, we are no longer in the convenient place of evading the issues. The Holy Spirit is pressing us relentlessly to address the false conceptions and sinful biases that have paralyzed some and dangerously fueled others. He is urging us now because the issues of prejudice and privilege have eroded the influence and authority of the church. Instead of leading the world in this issue, as Jesus did, the church in the United States has systematically yielded to economic, political, and cultural pressure on the issue of equality since our nation's earliest years.

At our nation's conception, the declaration was made: "We hold these truths to be self-evident, that all men are created equal, that they are endowed by their Creator with certain unalienable Rights, that among these are Life, Liberty and the pursuit of Happiness." Our nation's founders openly stated they believed in God. Yet, while they boldly declared, "All men are created equal," they failed to live up to their words. They capitulated on the issue of the equality of man, allowing southern states to edit out the rights of Black slaves from our Declaration of Independence for the sake of a unified voice against King George III. The original draft of the Declaration included the following phrase:

> He (King George) has waged cruel war against human nature itself, violating its most sacred rights of life and liberty in the persons of a distant people who never offended him, captivating and carrying them into slavery in another hemisphere, or to incur miserable death in their transportation thither (*ushistory.org*).

This statment, which powerfully condemned the practice of slavery, ended up being discarded because the southern colonies' full support for the American Revolution was pivotal to its success.

Our forefathers' ungodly and unbiblical concession regarding the equality of all men (and women) was born primarily on the literal backs of African slaves, Asian immigrants, and indigenous Americans. Giving immediate access and authority to a Satanic stronghold, this beast has continued to grip our nation in its claws. Our forefathers, as noble as they were in other areas, did not uphold Christ-like values regarding racism. With the sins of duplicity and acquiescence laid at the foundation of our country's beginnings, it is no wonder we continue to wrestle with issues of equality and justice today. The American elect of God still fight the tendency to bite their prophetic tongues instead of lifting their voices when it comes to race equity. Dr. Tony Evans addresses this eloquently:

> The fundamental cause of racial problems in America lies squarely with the church's failure. . . . Our failure to respond to this issue of Biblical oneness has allowed what never should have been a problem in the first place to continue for hundreds of years. . . . We cannot appeal to our heritage while simultaneously ignoring the moral inconsistencies…When we get it right in the church house is when we can spread it to the White House, and beyond.[4]

The same demonic spirit that deceived and intimidated our founding fathers continues to muffle our message and tarnish our testimony today—especially with the emerging generations. Our sons and daughters have little tolerance for double-tongued hypocrisy. These up-and-coming youth have absolutely no grace or patience, as previous generations did, to "wait just a little longer" for justice. Young people hold a deep hunger for an authentic and inclusive Gospel that reflects the Kingdom's values of justice, equity, and love. They would be so much more receptive to our messages regarding sexual purity and holy lifestyles if we would also uphold and defend race equality and justice toward people of color and the disenfranchised. We would have greater influence if we as a church were as easily motivated by the cries of the hurting and marginalized as we are by political power. (Yeah, I went there.)

AMERICAN JESUS

It's given me pause to consider what the Apostle Paul's reaction would be to the Christian nationalism that permeates some of our Gospel message in the United States. In certain circles, the American dream and the Gospel message have become diabolically fused together. Political influence, voting power, and wealth security are merged with issues such as abortion, gay marriage, and immigration, producing a congregational identity around shared political agendas and the bonding agent of its membership. God forbid an ignorant Sunday guest voice a differing political opinion or reveal they voted for the opposing party candidate. It would go better for them if they'd murdered someone the night before!

Though I am fiercely patriotic and deeply concerned over many of my country's current policies and laws, I am more troubled by this hybrid Christianity than who might be presently seated in the Oval Office, who controls the Congress, or who is appointed to the Supreme Court. If we are followers of Jesus Christ, no name should emblazon our banners but Christ's. We cannot allow ourselves to become so fixated on a person, a political party, or one righteous issue that we lose sight of our true and regal mission here on earth.

> "The kingdoms of this world have become the kingdoms of our Lord and of His Christ, and He shall reign forever and ever!" (Revelation 11:15 NKJV).

While being grateful for our nation and committing to serve our due diligence in the civic realm, we cannot forget our first and foremost allegiance is to the King of kings and His purposes in the world. Our primary citizenship is in heaven, not a nation. National zeal can never supersede our fidelity to the kingdom of God and His work on earth! Christ came not to establish an earthly government, but to save souls. A church that is divided down political and racial lines and disparaging each other in the pulpit and social media over differing political opinions weakens the influence and mission that Jesus entrusted to us. Jesus said, "Every kingdom divided against itself will be ruined, and every city or household divided against itself will not stand" (Matthew 12:25).

The juvenile social media quarreling, un-friending, and villainizing over political issues and candidates within the church has caused even the unsaved and unrighteous to step back appalled at our behavior. And, rightly so. For it is a heinous sin to allow the political or cultural division to disenfranchise us from the harvest field of souls. If the American church would put as much energy and money into saving souls as it does in saving our nation, our nation would certainly be saved!

We cannot trade the harvest field for the political field. Our association with a political party cannot surpass our loyalty for believing brothers and our passion for unity. Political identity must not corrupt our faith identity. Brother and sister believers in both political parties are all concerned about abortion, immigration, poverty, racial equity, and religious freedom. But by choosing loyalty to a party or a politician over the brotherhood of Jesus Christ, we diffuse the power of the Church's unified voice in these very areas. And we undermine the impact of our Gospel message to a multicultural audience. Each culture has its own political concerns and allegiances. So, when we as faith leaders promote—from our pulpits, in the public square, or on social media—a party, issue, or candidate, we immediately alienate an entire people group from our Gospel message.

Jesus repeatedly refused to align with revolutionary rhetoric against the corrupt, perverse, and violent government of Rome, even though his disciples hoped He would armor up and displace it. Instead, He focused on the promise and power of the Kingdom of God, displacing hell and its demons, healing the sick, and giving hope to the marginalized.

> Jesus said, "My kingdom is not of this world. If it were, my servants would fight to prevent my arrest by the Jewish leaders. But now my kingdom is from another place" (John 18:36).

A concerned chorus of courageous, wise, and prophetic voices has raised the alarm. Here are warnings from a few present-day notable leaders:

> God's kingdom does not allow for human government to either trump His rule or get so close to influencing His church that it weakens the church's distinctive nature, presence, or Biblical worldview operating in the culture.[5]
>
> To even suggest you cannot be a Christian unless you are a Republican or a Democrat, is to place one's political identity above one's faith in Jesus. No party sufficiently aligns with the kingdom of God.[6]
>
> American presidents last for 4 to 8 years. The Kingdom of God lasts forever. Yes, it matters who serves as president, but it's helpful to keep an eternal perspective as a Christian. Our hope is not ultimately in politics, and Christian witness in the process matters.[7]
>
> This Christian nationalism is not of God. Move back from it. . . . Fellow leaders, we will be held responsible for remaining passive in this day of seduction to save our own skin while the saints we've been entrusted to serve are being seduced, manipulated, used, and stirred up into a lather of zeal devoid of the Holy Spirit for political gain. . . . We do not place our faith in mortals. We are the church of the living God. . . . We have a king. His name is Jesus.[8]
>
> As long as what's Right or Left is more important to professing Christians than what is right or wrong, in light of Jesus, we are doomed to present a caricature of him to the world. Christ is neither left nor right nor is He centrist. God seated Him, "far above all rule and authority."[9]

German Lutheran pastor and theologian Dietrich Bonhoeffer, who was hanged by the Nazis in 1945, said, "One can't be a Christian and a nationalist at the same time."

The words of Dr. Martin Luther King, speaking in his 1967 Christmas sermon on peace, still ring true for us today: "If we are to have peace on earth, our loyalties must become ecumenical rather than sectional. Our loyalties must transcend our race, our tribe, our class, and our nation."

The Lord is not on the side of any politician or party. He has not registered as a Democrat or Republican. He's not on the side of Black people, Brown people, Asian people, or White people. He's on His own side! It reminds me of Joshua's posture shifting encounter with the Lord of Hosts when surveying Jericho:

> Now when Joshua was near Jericho, he looked up and saw a man standing in front of him with a drawn sword in his hand. Joshua went up to him and asked, "Are you for us or for our enemies?" "Neither," he replied, "but as commander of the army of the Lord I have now come." Then Joshua fell facedown to the ground in reverence, and asked him, "What message does my Lord have for his servant?" The commander of the Lord's army replied, "Take off your sandals, for the place where you are standing is holy." And Joshua did so (Joshua 5:13-15).

Like Joshua, it behooves us to fall on our faces, take off our shoes, and lower our swords. Only then will the Jericho walls of injustice, racism, abortion, perversion, corruption, and materialism fall in our nation. Unity conferences and racial reconciliation gatherings have taken place globally over the years. Preachers preach about it and position papers are written. Though certainly inspiring, we must admit too little has been accomplished in conquering the territory of racism and prejudice held by the devil for generations. That is because *going there* requires much more from us. It involves taking a good hard look at our own hard hearts and inexcusable excuses for systemic prejudice that crushes hope, quashes dreams, and snuffs out lives.

Going there is very personal. It is a heart-formed conviction that prompts the passionate dismantling of all contrary to Christ's kingdom values in our lives. And it "won't happen in the White house until it happens in the church house." But, it can't happen in the church house until it happens first in you and me.

Endnotes

1. David A. Anderson, *Gracism: The Art of Inclusion* (Intervarsity Press, 2007)
2. Trillia J. Newbell, *United: Captured by God's Vision for Diversity* (Moody Publishers, 2014)
3. Genesis 1:27, *Strong's Hebrew Concordance*; (Adam—*Baker's Evangelical Dictionary of Biblical Theology*)
4. Tony Evans, *Oneness Embraced* (Moody Publishers, 2015)
5. Evans, *Oneness Embraced*
6. @tweetraychang 11/17/ 2020
7. @tweetraychang 11/4/2020
8. @BethMooreLPM Twitter 12/13/20
9. @BethMooreLPM Twitter 1/09/21

II. THE MOTIVATION

The reason or reasons one has for acting or behaving in a particular way; the general desire or willingness of someone to do something.

4

What's Love Got to Do With It?

We sat together in my office: he forlornly sank into the cushy couch, and I sat across from him in a large chair. Untouched mugs of coffee steamed on the table between us. Surveying his sunken posture and tense facial features, it was unmistakably apparent the youthful zeal of this young pastor had disintegrated into dismay. Normally energetic and fast-talking, he was now subdued and pensive. His first year as the lead pastor had knocked the stuffing right out of him. His newly found humility wasn't necessarily a bad thing if it was used as a catalyst for personal growth. It was my hope he would *fail forward.*

His melancholy caused me to reflect on my first pastorate. I'd left my hometown and my father's thriving ministry to lead a small church in Southern California with 17 elderly members and a 30-year history of pastoral turnovers. Undaunted by these facts, I jumped into the new assignment enthusiastically, wishing to prove myself a worthy leader. With "visions of sugar plums dancing in my head," my visionary aspirations were quickly trampled by a nightmarish herd of realities. I returned home after six crushing years, mirroring the dejection of this young pastor now slumped on the sofa in front of me.

After listening to his long list of frustrations and vexations, he looked intently into my eyes, and implored, "What's wrong, Pastor? Why can't I build this church?"

The reason for my son-in-the-faith's lack of ministerial success was obvious to me, recognizable only because the Lord had previously allowed my failures to sift me. Much like the Apostle Peter prior to Christ's death, my ministry had been ego-based, not love-based. Though I had prided myself in being a passionate follower and minister of Jesus, it was frustration, fatigue, and failure that finally illuminated the truth: too much of my passion was contingent on His leading me to prominence and position. My faith and leadership had been wide-eyed with enthusiasm yet operated from self-centered and self-serving motivations. I'd come into that little church like a tiny tornado, with very little concern for the history and heart of the remaining saints who had sacrificed and endured in hope for a future harvest. Though the church initially grew in number, the inevitable fires of crisis and opposition laid bare my true impulses. I was not serving for the betterment of the people, but for the advancement of my call.

My decision-making through trial was self-motivated, not love motivated. So, as the congregation began to decrease and leadership quietly slipped away, I found myself much in the same condition as my young mentee: frustrated, angry, and bewildered. A wise and straight-talking ministry veteran offered an undiluted challenge to me: "Do you love the people?" she asked.

I snorted, "What's love got to do with it?"

"Okay, Tina Turner! It has to do with everything. If you don't understand that, maybe you shouldn't be pastoring," she countered.

Ouch. "Faithful are the wounds of a friend" (Proverbs 27:6 KJV).

FAILING FORWARD

We all initially answer the call of Christ somewhat starry-eyed and propelled by self-interest. In Peter's case, he quickly left his slimy fishing nets at Jesus' invitation to become a "fisher of men" (Matthew 4:18-22 NKJV). We honor Peter's bold decision to follow Christ. Yet, I imagine, when he looked down at the smelly fish and then at his perspiration-soaked and equally smelly fishing buddies, I doubt his motivation was completely saintly and selfless. We see consistently Peter's brash and self-promoting behavior until his humiliating abandonment and renouncement of Jesus (Matthew 26:31-35, 69-75). He squabbled with the other disciples continuously about placement and prominence (20:28). They collectively had great difficulty with the concept of forgiveness (18:21-22). Children were more of a nuisance to the boys in Jesus' band than a blessing (18:15-17). Christ's fixation on sinners and outcasts was perplexing, as was His unnerving fondness for Samaritans. Topping all this was Jesus completely ignoring their ultimate aspiration of ousting the Romans from Israel. Peter argued with Jesus about His impending suffering because it did not fit his plans (16:21-24). Peter's service was as much about his private agenda, as it was about Christ's kingdom. Shallow faith and self-centeredness were fully evidenced when his perception of Jesus and himself shattered at Gethsemane (26:47-54). Jesus warned Peter at the Last Supper:

> "Simon, Simon! Indeed, Satan has asked for you, that he may sift you as wheat. But I have prayed for you, that your faith should not fail; and when you have returned to Me, strengthen your brethren." But he said to Him, "Lord, I am ready to go with You, both to prison and to death." Then He said, "I tell you, Peter, the rooster shall not crow this day before you will deny three times that you know Me" (Luke 22:31-34 NKJV).

It is comforting to know Jesus already knew the fragility of Peter's faith and followership. Therefore, Christ was not horrified or surprised by his impending abandonment, cursing, and denial. Thankfully, our Lord is not shocked or appalled when you and I blow it either. (You can shout "Hallelujah!" here). Yet intrinsic to Jesus' revelation to Peter (and to us) is the reality that God cannot and will not allow His called ones to stay shallow, hyper-religious, egocentric, or biased. He will lead us to lead for love's sake. For this reason, Christ allowed Satan to sift Peter. For this reason, He allows us also to be sifted.

SHAKEN, NOT STIRRED

The word *sift* means to separate particles—take something out, examine, or pass through. The picture here reminds me of how my Grandma Phoebe would sift flour before baking her yummy pies. She would take cups of flour I thought looked just fine, and pour them through a sifter. Shaking it vigorously, what emerged was fine and silken. The result was the most delicious crusts known to mankind, but the flour underwent trauma in the process, as did the kitchen! Flour was everywhere and on everyone. To those of us who stuffed our mouths with scrumptious cherry pie, it was well worth the transitory mess.

This "sifting scene" closely resembled what God does with us. He uses failure, frustration, crisis, and disappointment to separate the particles of pretension from pure silken faith. He forcefully shakes us until the lumpy and noncompliant bits surrender to a smooth consistency. Our lives undergo trauma and look like grandma's messy kitchen, but the result is a palatable faith and message, full of texture, flavor and packed with genuine sustenance for those who are hungry and thirsty for the authentic Gospel. Through failure, Peter's shallow ministry motivations were sifted to become appetizing to a hungry and lost world.

SELECTED FOR SIFTING

God has a holy habit of sifting and shaking those He has selected. There are numerous examples of this concept in Scripture besides Peter. Here are a few more memorable sifted and shaken individuals.

Joseph. His youthful vision of his family bowing down to him had prophetic impetus. Yet that dream had to be stripped of its self-serving perspective. So, Joseph's faith was tested in a pit ... then tested again in the house of Potiphar ... and finally again in an Egyptian prison. Through those agonizing and bewildering circumstances, God redefined both Joseph's dream and his faith. Oh yes, his family would bow to him, because God would promote Joseph to second-in-command in Egypt. Yet, God was not promoting him to rule over his father and brothers as he first thought. The promotion was so he could save and serve them. (see Genesis 37-45). *Joseph's struggles sifted the egotism out of his dream.*

Moses. As a Hebrew babe, Moses was miraculously saved from death and delivered into the arms of an Egyptian princess. He grew up in Pharaoh's court as part of the royal family and was educated as a prince. When of age, he realized his Hebrew ancestry and became incensed over the unjust and harsh treatment of his people. Zeal distorted into a murderous rage against an Egyptian slave-master, and Moses killed him. Running for his life, Moses found himself in the Midian desert shepherding the sheep belonging to his future father-in-law. So traumatized was Moses during these dark and hopeless days, he began to stutter. Nonetheless, God had a purpose in the pain. He promoted Moses so he could return to Egypt as the Hebrew's deliverer and transport them triumphant to the shores of a Promised Land. (See Exodus 2-3.) *Moses' failings sifted entitlement from his call.*

The Apostle Paul. Before Paul became the apostle to the Gentiles, he was an ambitious and religious man named Saul. Saul's religious and nationalistic fervor boiled into bigotry against Jesus' followers, causing him to rise in influence among the Jewish leadership of the Sanhedrin. On assignment to Damascus to assault and persecute Christians, God provided Saul with a tailor-made "dark time." Jesus literally knocked Paul off his high horse, struck him blind, confronted his deception, and rerouted his self-aggrandizing mission. The confrontation, humiliation, and isolation of his blinding experience reshaped his faith and his identity from Saul, the self-promoting religious zealot, to Paul, Jesus' bridge to the Gentile people. (See Acts 9.) *Paul's fall sifted religion from revelation.*

Simon Peter. Peter's failure sifted his faith to such humble surrender that even with the knowledge there would be no throne or riches for him in this world, he emerged to meekly lead the early church with Christ-wrought love and power. Jesus' gentle question over a fish breakfast would not only be Peter's restoration but also would clarify the motivation for Peter's ministry. "Do you love me? . . . then feed my sheep" (John 21:15-17). Love had everything to do with it. At Peter's initial calling, Jesus had appealed to him to follow and become a "fisher of men." Fish, for Peter, was a source of personal sustenance and an identity marker. But now, Jesus was challenging Peter not to *feed off* the sheep, but, instead, to *feed* the sheep. Peter would no longer catch people for his own purpose but, like Jesus, would give up his life for them (vv. 18-20). The motivation for this paradigm shift would be love. According to church history, Peter would punctuate this call by dying a martyr's death on his own inverted cross.

Today we hear of Jesus, His love for us, His amazing sacrifice on the cross, and His powerful resurrection from His encounter with a brash, egocentric, cursing fisherman named Simon who was sifted until he became the love-led, humble, yet courageous man called Peter. *Peter's failure sifted pretention from his purpose.*

Struggle, failure, and pain are how God sifts the "me" out of our motivations. For the church, crisis, pandemic, persecution, economic struggle, moral failing, rifts, and division are used by God to sift the "us" and "them" into the "we" and "our." The question is not if God is sifting His leaders and church right now. Instead, the question is, will we hold onto the fibrous fragments of pride that divide us, or will we humble ourselves and submit to His sifting and blending?

MOTIVATIONS MATTER

"Pastor Rae, did you hear me?" my mentee queried, interrupting my reflections.

"What's wrong?" he asked again, "Why can't I build this church?"

"Dear one, I could give you some practical and strategic suggestions, but these things are not your real issue."

He tapped his fingers on the sofa seat, contemplating whether he wanted to hear the "real issue." But much to his credit, he collected his courage and said, "Okay, then. What's the real issue?"

"The real issue is you don't love the people. You don't even like them. In fact, it seems you can barely tolerate them. You love the concept of ministry but not its purpose–that is, people.

These precious people in your congregation are simply a means for you to practice and platform your gifting."

His eyes moistened, but he needed the principle to be more specific, so I continued.

"When you preach, do you think about what they need to hear or what *you* want to say? As you organize the church do consider what will build them up or lift *you* up?"

I paused until the initial sting had passed. He didn't answer the questions. Instead, he whispered painfully, "But I thought God told me to go there."

"He did," I affirmed. "He did call you there. But *there* is usually not where we think it is." Peter discovered "there" was not on a golden throne next to Jesus, but a breakfast of brokenness on the shore of the Sea of Galilee. "I think you're *there* now, my son. God wants to use this failure not to crush you, but so you'll be fueled by a more powerful motivation. Love must be the motivator for all you do. Because we can never win what we don't love. *For it is love that compels our 'go'!"*

Motivation refers to the reason or reasons one has for acting or behaving in a particular way—the general desire or willingness of someone to do something. When John 3:16 says, "For God so loved the world . . ." it is more than a righteous reflection. His love for us motivated and provoked astonishing action. Love compelled Jesus to set aside His heavenly culture, strip off His glorious and radiant immortality, and replaced it with humanity's skin—skin that sunburned, calloused, wrinkled, bled, and decayed. He immersed Himself in our culture—wearing our clothing, eating our food, sweating alongside us in work, resting His holy head on our pillows, attending our feeble festivals and ceremonies. How pale it all must have been compared to Heaven's glory. Yet, He loved so greatly, He came and became one of us. He loved so greatly He endured the cross for our restoration and went the extra mile for our reconciliation. He loved us so greatly, He took the penalty for our rebellion and corruption. He loved so greatly, Christ held the devil accountable for crushing our souls and lifted us with His resurrection. He did not do it for glory or our validation. He did not do it for a throne or a crown. Love and only love was His great motivator. Love must be our motivation as well.

God will put us in His grip of grace. He will squeeze us through frustration, failure, crisis, and disappointment until, like sponges soaked in rancid water, the selfishness forcibly dribbles out. Cleansed by tears of surrender, our vision will be renewed and our gaze refocused. Suddenly, what had seemed to be a menace becomes our mission field.

"I tell you, open your eyes and look at the fields! They are ripe for harvest" (John 4:35), Jesus said to his astonished disciples as Samaritans streamed to the well from the town. They had gone dutifully into Sychar, motivated primarily by their own appetites, but Jesus would teach them to be driven by love.

REPELLED OR COMPELLED?

It was my habit to walk around our Tucson church's 10-acre inner-city campus at least weekly. This routine gave me a chance to stretch my legs, pray, and check on how our facilities staff was keeping things up. On this chilly afternoon, my pace displayed my misery as I dragged around the block and tearfully complained to the Lord. It was more of a gripe session than a prayer session. My first two years into the pastorate were as though I'd been dropped from a helicopter into a war zone. We'd inherited a monstrous debt, navigated a contentious lawsuit, and dealt with former staff exploiting the pastoral transition to split the church. Most devastating to me personally had been the brutal betrayal of family members. Sadness engulfed me and I found it difficult to preach, lead meetings, or counsel—all tasks that had once been a joy.

Heartbroken, I planned to resign. Though we had seen considerable growth and spiritual fruit, drawing people from all over the city, I didn't possess the stamina, courage, or the incentive to continue. Slowly rounding the corner of the gym, I was stunned out of my blubbering into a horrified halt. Large, crude, spray-painted gang symbols defaced the sidewalk and building. Disgusted at the disrespect of the taggers who had likely been the vandals, I began to formulate a plan to keep them all out. I quickened my pace back to the offices while complaining to God aloud:

"These little brats! No respect for your house! No fear of You!" I grumbled. "Well, I'd wanted an open campus but obviously, that's not possible in this neighborhood or with these people! We'll put up signs this week: no loitering, no skateboarding, no, no, no! We'll finish the fencing and lock the gates until service times. We'll put up cameras on the corners and increase the security presence. I know how to keep them out!"

"I WANT THEM HERE!" The voice that rumbled within stopped me suddenly. I stood still, trying to explain away what I knew was the thundering of God's Spirit echoing in the hallways of my heart.

"What? Lord?" I breathed cautiously.

"I want them here," He said again, then commanded, "TAG THEM BACK!"

Unforgettable was this moment for the church and for me. The idea that God wanted these neighborhood renegades roaming the sacred sanctum of the church property was unimaginable. *What in the world is God up to?* I wondered. I was soon to discover He was meddling with my ministry motivations, and lifting my eyes from my woes to a harvest of souls that moved His heart.

LOVE ATTRACTION

What causes us to recoil in disgust, attracts Jesus. What we avoid, He is drawn to. What we shun, He embraces. Jesus usually has a different response to sinners than we do. He is attracted to them. Drawn, pulled, and moved, He stoops down not only to walk on our dirt and through our filth, He reaches out His holy hand to touch it. He touches our arrogance, hypocrisy, unfaithfulness, sickness, sin, and even our death. It is as though He is attracted to the lack, the need, the mess, the misery, and the void.

Jesus, the Good Shepherd, will leave the 99 content, safe, and strong to find the one wayward straggler, according to Matthew 18:12. He stayed up late at night to connect with a curious and self-righteous Pharisee, Nicodemus, in John 3. He stood up for a humiliated adulterous in John 8. Jesus stopped everything to respond to the frantic cry of a blind man in Matthew 10:46. He defied rabbinic tradition to lay His life-giving hand on a widow's dead son in Luke 7:11-17. Christ paused at a sycamore tree to call a conniving thief, Zacchaeus, out of his hiding place in Luke 19:1-10. He went out of His way to reach a humiliated adulterous woman in John 4. It was a love attraction. In the same

HE HAD TO GO THERE

way, the Spirit of God was attracted to the void, the nothingness of the earth in Genesis 1:2, Jesus is drawn to empty and formless places of our hearts.

Genesis 1:2 says, "Now the earth was formless and empty, darkness was over the surface of the deep, and the Spirit of God was hovering over the waters." God's Spirit hovers over humanity's need and is pulled to the places of darkness, hopelessness, and desperation.

What does this have to do with us? There are over 330 million people in the United States alone. The vast majority of these are hopelessly lost and without Christ's love. What shall we do? We've "made" it already, and the mission is messy. As the throng of sinners increases and the global culture becomes more confusing and seemingly unreachable, in frustration, we as Christians too often shut in and shut down. We are tempted to fence in our campuses or move to more pleasant neighborhoods. It is agreeably simpler to fashion our churches as refuges for the godly, not embassies for the lost, with programs, language ("Christianese"), fellowship, and music suited to our liking. Our focus then is on ourselves, rather than being attracted and prompted toward, as Jesus was, to the need.

Cornel West—a philosopher, civil-rights activist, and son of a Baptist preacher—encapsulated this principle when he said, "You can't lead the people if you don't love the people. You can't save the people if you don't serve the people" (*www.cornelwest.com*).

TAG, YOU'RE IT

I'll never forget the dropped jaws and flabbergasted expressions of the pastoral staff and church council when I announced Jesus wanted us to invite the gang kids onto our property and

What's Love Got to Do With It?

into our ministry. Redirected by the need and revitalized by vision, my eyes had been lifted and my heart purposefully shifted from my sorrows to the pain of others. Compassion fueled me as I laid out the strategy that would strain our budget, press our leadership, and test our resolve. One elder warned, "This could ruin us!"

Yep! It's risky stuff, this Great Commission. Yet, once we were united in purpose and had collaborated on a plan, we found it was all so very worth it. Instead of closing the campus, we flung the gates wide. Over the next year, we opened the gym for sports and renovated old offices for after-school tutoring, family and immigration counseling, and refugee ministries. Businesses and church people gave liberally toward flat-screen TVs, gaming consoles, game tables, sofas, desks, and computers. Teachers, school nurses, social workers, veterans, artists, coaches, musicians, and retirees staffed our volunteer army. We offered counseling, family fun nights, food, and financial aid. The word got out, and the property flooded with skateboarding, basketball, game-playing youth, and their grateful parents. The latter were more work than their children! It was a marvelous, messy miracle.

We did lose a few indignant church families who did not want to sit next to baggy jeaned hoodlums on Sundays, or their teenager worshiping with neighborhood kids at youth group. Yet, we gained a community of souls. Ironically, there was no more tagging. *We had tagged them back.*

We don't go to those Jesus is attracted to simply because we don't love them enough. As with Jesus' disciples, we often become so focused on our agendas and struggles, we hardly give a glance to those that captivate Christ's attention. Like the disciples foraging for food in Sychar, we miss our mission because we're so caught up in our ministry assignment. Christ has His way of refocusing our gaze. He will repurpose our personal and corporate pain and problems to sift our hearts until our only motivation for ministry is love. Because we will only win what we love. Second Corinthians 5:14 reads, "For Christ's love compels us, because we are convinced that one died for all."

Love compels the "go."

5

Going Back for the Future

"I'm sick of it!" Jim burst out. His round, wrinkled face was flushing pink in aggravation. "The Blacks, Indians, Mexicans, and Orientals—they are always talking about things that happened in the past. They keep trying to force me to think about and repent for something I didn't do. I don't have slaves. I'm not in the KKK! I didn't take any Indian land. I didn't kick an illegal out of America! Why can't they let it go? Why can't we just move on already!" he bellowed, slapping his hand on the table with such force, it propelled the silverware, coffee cups, and plates an inch into the air. His long-suffering wife, Helen, jumped up and proceeded to clean up the coffee and crumbs that had been rocketed from their receptacles.

"Jim, calm down!" she demanded sternly.

He quieted himself with a big sigh that emanated from his very soul.

"I'm sorry, Pastor, I get so worked up about this—it makes me mad. I don't understand why we keep having to go back to the past and talk about it. Can't we leave it all back there?"

Jim and Helen were lovely people. They had raised a family, built a local business, and faithfully served in their community church together for literally decades. Dinner in the charming home of this older couple had, until this point, been especially pleasant. That is until the subject of race relations in the area and the recent protests came up. Jim's demeanor had suddenly shifted from charming to alarming! I sat back in my chair wondering if it was time to make a swift exit. Yet the subject was too important for cowardice, even if it meant braving an enormous, aggravated man like Jim on his home turf. There was also Helen's famous homemade apple pie on my plate to bolster my courage. So, with a combination of sugar rush and the Holy Spirit, I dared to poke the bear.

"So why not continue to talk about this issue if it helps the healing and brings changes, Brother Jim?" I prodded.

"Because it's in the past and it needs to stay there!" he thundered.

"Jim, I said, calm down!" Helen appeared frail, but I wouldn't cross her.

Jim collected himself at her command as I silently prayed for Holy Spirit's help. Helen refilled my coffee. Prayer, caffeine, and sugar: armed and ready.

"Brother Jim, do you remember that old movie *Back to the Future*?" I explored carefully.

"Yeah, we love that movie!" they said in chorus, distracted by my seeming shift in topic.

"I love it too!" I smiled. "It's one of my favorites—but we're all really dating ourselves now!" We laughed together in agreement. Then I continued.

"The last scene is the most profound, isn't it? Because Marty McFly time-traveled back to the '50s and emboldened his timid teenage father, the entire McFly family was transformed in the future. His dad became a famous book writer instead of Biff the Bully's car-washer. *Sometimes we have to go back for the sake of the future."*

They nodded politely, not yet grasping the principle.

"Your oldest son walks with a limp, doesn't he?" I probed.

"Yeah, why?" Jim now eyed me warily, but I stayed quiet, hoping the pause would provoke further explanation from him.

A few moments passed, then he explained, "He was on his bike coming home from school and was hit by a drunk driver. He was just a boy—so young and full of life. It . . . it was terrible."

"Do you occasionally talk with your son about that day, Brother Jim?" I asked.

"Sometimes," he said quietly.

"How old is he now?" I queried.

Helen interjected, "He's 43."

Jim didn't hear her. He was time-traveling, translated back 30 years to the sights and sounds of that awful day.

"Why?" I ventured.

"Why do we talk about it? Because what happened that day changed my boy's life forever. He's all grown up with kids of his own now, but when I see him walk in the door with that limp, it still hurts me. His leg and hip were crushed. He was in a cast for a year, and there were so many surgeries right up into his teens. He couldn't play baseball, climb trees, or ride his bike like his friends. He fell behind in school. He got robbed of so much, and it wasn't even his fault. You know, my wife and I went every day to the trial of the drunk who hit him. We even did—whattaya call it, Helen?"

"A victim statement," Helen answered.

"Yeah, that's it. It was really important to us that man was held accountable for what he did to our son. We don't hate him, but he needed to be accountable for what he did, right?

"Absolutely!" I nodded in agreement. "It wasn't about hate or unforgiveness. You needed justice!"

Jim's eyes now shone with pride and love. The grievous memories dissolved into warm reflection, and his voice gentled. "I really love my boy. You know, as he grew, I always made an extra effort to help him move forward as a man. And he has! He's a wonderful husband and father. I'm so proud of him and I love him so much." His eyes moistened, and his wife reached over and held his hand.

This was my cue. "You love him, and that's why you still feel the hurt! That's why you are still willing to talk about that day with him when he needs to. That's why it was important to you the man who hit him was held accountable. You grieve the childhood losses and go the extra mile for him, even though he's full grown. You do it because of love, and you'd do it again, right?"

They both nodded vigorously and then fell silent. I reached over and put my hand on Jim's burly arm, and then continued.

"So, let's go there, Brother Jim. Just as you do with your son, it's necessary to go back and process pain and inequity with people. We do it because we love them. If we, our ancestors, or our nation, participated in the hurt and the hate, love asks that we own up to that injustice. Even if we don't think we were the ones who personally caused their pain; even if the original wound happened decades or generations before, the violation still causes a limp, and love prompts us to address it. Love makes us tireless in standing up as many times as necessary to say it was wrong. Because doing so heals hearts, dignifies souls, brings justice, and motivates change. Acknowledging wrong that was done is a powerful thing, not only for the person who was impacted but also for those who did the hurting.

"When your son was hit by that drunk, you didn't sweep it under the rug or tell your boy to move on and get over it. No! It was necessary to bring accountability. That's why you did the victim statement and attended the trial. Not to exact vengeance, but so your precious son would always know what happened that day wasn't right and help all of you process it. I bet that trial happened a long time after the incident too. Love is always willing to go back, no matter how far, so others can move forward.

"There's a whole lot of beautiful people out there who walk with a limp because they were run down by prejudice and racism—some of them, literally. These discussions, unity conferences, and even those protests are victim statements that need to be told and acknowledged. Because of love, we should listen. Because of love, we should acknowledge it too. If need be, repeatedly, until all the racists are off the street. Because we love, we go back for the sake of the future."

TAKE ME BACK, DEAR LORD

The journey up the rocky path toward Sychar in Samaria had most likely been exhausting. Feeling the growl of empty stomachs after the morning's hot hike, the disciples were sent by Jesus into the town of Sychar to buy lunch. Finally free of His disciples' incessant bickering and questioning, Jesus wearily seated himself by the well just outside the town.

> Jacob's well was there, and Jesus, tired as he was from the journey, sat down by the well. It was about noon. When a Samaritan woman came to draw water, Jesus said to her, "Will you give me a drink?" (His disciples had gone into the town to buy food.) (John 4:6-8).

This was not the first time God had been here. Some seventeen centuries prior, just twenty or so miles away, our gracious God met Jacob, a desperate young man running in terror from his brother, Esau. All alone at night in that arid isolated place, with only a rock for a pillow, Jacob dreamed of a ladder that led to Heaven. It changed the trajectory of his life (Genesis 28:10-21). The hilly landscape of this region would draw Jacob back repeatedly during his lifetime to worship, build altars, and dig wells. We read of Jacob's return to the area with his herds, wives, sons, and one precious daughter, named Dinah. Jacob dug a well in this place; a well that not only gave physical refreshing but also reminded the family of God's gracious overflow of blessing and favor.

Now Jesus, God incarnate—the "living ladder" of Jacob's dream—positioned Himself at that historic well. It had endured as a source of natural water but had long since ceased to be a symbol of spiritual refreshing and revelation. Spiritually it had been filled with the debris of shame—poisoned by lust, religious deception, violence, and injustice through the years. The poisoning of this spiritual wellspring began with the diggers, Jacob and his sons. In their time, the small town of Sychar was called "Shechem," named after the young Canaanite prince who lived within its gates. Prince Shechem eyed Jacob's beautiful young daughter, Dinah, with a lustful leer. Overcome, he abducted and raped her. Enraged by Dinah's violation and their father's apparent apathy for justice, her brothers took vengeance into their own hands. It culminated in the massacre of every father and son in the city (Genesis 30:21; 34; 46:15).

The rampage satiated the brothers' blood-lust, so Jacob and his sons moved on. But Dinah remained captive to the trauma: shame-ridden, loveless, childless, and empty for the rest of her life. Though her name means "vindication," there would be none. Until the day Jesus stepped onto the dirt and dust of that sin-soiled terrain. He went back there—to the exact landscape and the same well. He waited knowingly and intentionally for a woman who, like Dinah, was devastated by sexual sin, shame-filled, lonely, and degraded. She traversed the dusty path in the heat of the day, with an empty pot on her head, poignantly reflecting the hollowness of her heart. Parched in body and soul, she lowered her vessel once again to fill it with tepid, stale water that never satisfied.

"May I have a drink?" Jesus asked her.

But He never takes a drink! Instead, He offers her a drink—the living water of a relationship with God. She is transformed and restored. She finds such dignity and joy it overflows into the town, and the Samaritans come, like a tidal wave, toward the well. God went back to the well of Sychar so a woman, a people, and a region could have a future with Him. He went back to redeem Dinah's shame by liberating the Samaritan woman and her people. He went back to redeem Jacob's passivity with His intentionality. He went back to replace deceit with truth, division with inclusion, religion with relationship, and *racism with "gracism."* (*Gracism* is a term created by author David A. Anderson.)

To reach and lead people groups who have experienced the identity crushing of prejudice and racism, we must be willing, as Jesus was, to reach back into the places of pain and the incidents of injustice. In doing so, we recognize the collective and individual trauma in its ugly reality, without dilution or defense. Sincere repentance, even when representational, paves the way for restoration and validates personal and cultural worth, rebuilding relational bridges to reconciliation and Kingdom partnership. We can do this practically by learning and then acknowledging the historical and present prejudices of ministries we are a part of; by calling racism "sin" in its every form; by teaching and preaching God's value of diversity from our pulpits and platforms, and by personally going back in repentance and reconciliation

For those who have not been impacted by soul-crushing experiences of prejudice, rehearsing what might be considered by some as bygone injustices seems like an unnecessary regurgitation of unpleasant history. Yet for those who have been racism's targets, it is immensely healing, validating, and elevating, enabling hearts to engage a greater purpose and rebuild Kingdom relationships.

ROBES OF RECONCILIATION

A close friend and fellow minister we'll call "Juan" told me of a life-changing event that involved *going back*. Growing up in Mexico, Juan's parents were powerful Latino ministers, traveling the nation to preach to indigenous people groups, plant churches, and establish Bible schools. The adventures he and his siblings experienced while accompanying their parents on Gospel exploits seem straight out of storybook fiction. They told wild tales of crossing rivers, trudging down snake-filled paths, and sleeping in huts to share the love of Jesus with the unreached. The gutsy faith of his parents was astounding. They pressed past daily danger and demonic resistance, and stood strong in the face of vicious persecution. Persecution came from "witchdoctors" who conjured up spells and fomented hysteria. Yet the most ominous threat arose from Catholic priests who resorted to targeted violence in their attempts to expel the missionaries. So aggressive were their measures, the family barely survived mobs, hut-burning, stoning, and poisoning, let alone constant slanderous accusations meant to cripple their ministry.

The memories of these events, and the pious unapologetic faces of the priests who instigated the attacks, became seared upon Juan's mind. Even the sound of a priest's rustling robes made him bristle. Though he now led a thriving Latino congregation in the United States, he maintained an aversion to Catholics as a whole, but especially to priests. Until the day one daring and determined priest went back for the sake of restoration and reconciliation. It happened at a ministers' conference. Pastor Juan and several of his peers in the Latino community were encouraged to attend. Planning to meet early and sit together, my friend's intentions were frustrated by morning traffic. Getting into the auditorium late, he realized almost every chair was filled, and the auditorium packed. As the first morning speaker was introduced, Juan spied an empty seat just two rows from the front and hurried down the aisle to claim it. So focused on getting settled, Juan didn't notice his neighbor was a Catholic priest, already seated in the chair next to his. To hear Pastor Juan tell the story of how he jumped when he turned and saw the priest in his religious garb, the panic that ensued, and the flushing and perspiration, cannot be matched by my words here!

Regardless of Juan's horror, he was trapped there for the entire day. All he could think of is why Catholics were even invited to this event. After all, *Are they really saved*?

After a day of power-packed sessions, the event director came to the podium to close the conference. The man announced his plan for the conclusion: The attendees would all connect with the person sitting next to them, confess their sins, and pray for one another. Anxiety now surged through my friend as he tried to quickly leave, but the aisles were jammed with praying partners. He was trapped! The priest smiled at him, sensing Juan's struggle, but purposefully moved toward him.

"I've been hoping to talk with you all day," the priest said. " I'm so glad we have this moment."

I'm not, Pastor Juan thought. *I want outta here. It's one thing to forgive, but it's another thing to let this guy pray for me!*

The priest, however, wasn't moving. He stepped close to Juan, robes rustling as he moved. Putting his hand on Juan's shoulder, he began to confess to the cruelty, persecution, and hate his brother priests had perpetrated on Protestant missionaries in Latin American countries. No excuses were made. Nor did the priest minimize the brutality, its lasting impact, or disparage the character of the recipients of the hate. This priest named it all as sinful and undeserved. He then humbly asked forgiveness from Pastor Juan for what his church and brotherhood had done.

Juan recounted trying to hold down emotion as the priest meekly and candidly recited the atrocities that had scarred Juan's soul since childhood. Like a dam that had been breached, Juan erupted into sobs that shook his whole body. The priest embraced Pastor Juan, and they wept together. Hurt and hate dissolved into wonder and laughter. As he stepped back and shook the priest's hand, Juan realized the despised priestly robes were saturated with his own tears. They had been transformed from robes of religion to robes of reconciliation that day.

Juan avows when walking out of the auditorium that evening, he felt taller, freer, and stronger than he had before. Amazingly, Pastor Juan's ministry immediately began to attract Catholics and even former priests—people who were looking for a simple and authentic message of love and forgiveness. Pastor Juan became a healed healer. His influence expanded so greatly, the professor of religious studies at the state university, a Catholic priest, scheduled him annually to share the lecture and teach. *Going back had catapulted Pastor Juan forward.*

DRINK UP

The power of this Biblical principle is illuminated through the establishment of Jubilee for God's people in Leviticus 25:9-10. Every fiftieth year, Israel would celebrate the year of Jubilee. It allowed for a new beginning in each generation. Those who had sold lands, gone into debt, or been given into servitude, had lands restored, debts canceled, and slaves set free at Jubilee. Jubilee was a time of magnificent celebration, restoration, and renewal of relationships, inheritance, and hope. Announced by the trumpeting of the ram's horn, feasting commenced, and new wine flowed. However, Israel could not celebrate Jubilee without participating first in the Day of Atonement—a period of introspection and repentance. On the Day of Atonement, known as *Yom Kippur*, the people of Israel were, and still are, encouraged to go back to make amends and ask forgiveness for sins committed during the past year. Only then, when sins had been confessed, wrongs righted, and atonement made, could the Jubilee party begin. They had to first sip the cup of repentance before drinking the cup of Jubilee.[1]

The principle prevails when reconciling with those who have been marginalized by prejudice. Jemar Tisby states: "Jumping ahead to the victories means skipping the hard but necessary work of examining what went wrong with race and the church."[2] We cannot gulp down Jubilee's lavish cup of reconciliation and reunification without first going back to sip the bitter cup of repentance.

While Jesus was hanging in agony on the cross, He asked the same question as He did of the Samaritan woman at Jacob's well: "May I have a drink?" (see John 19:28). Once again, His thirst was not for water; it was for souls! He thirsted that you and I would drink the cup of salvation He so liberally poured out. He went back, willing to physically revisit the foul and fetid well of humanity's sin for the sake of our future.

Where once God had walked with mankind in the Garden of Eden, Jesus stepped back into a garden—Gethsemane. There Christ initiated His final confrontation with the historic curse that turned the domain of God's blessing into a field of thorns. He then, at the cross, defeated the sin, death, and grave that had claimed generation after generation. Many believe He even went back all the way to hell to proclaim redemption to its prisoners there (see 1 Peter 3:18-20). We could not claim justice and peace for ourselves, so He went back on our behalf and broke the curse, covering every past, present, and future sin, lifting us into victory. God's purposed future was secured for us because Jesus went back. Our destiny as a unified Church awaits us if we too will *go back*.

Endnotes

1. Inspired by Tony Evans, *Oneness Embraced*
2. Jemar Tisby, *The Color of Compromise: The Truth about the American Church's Complicity in Racism (Zondervan, 2020)*

6

Let's Kill This Giant

My son, Pierce, screamed in pain and ran toward me, with a parade of preschoolers following him. They had all, just moments prior, been happily playing together at the park playground. We "mommies" were sitting together at the nearest picnic table, watching over our children and catching up with each other.

"Dillon bit me!" my son screamed.

Sure enough, upon inspection, the indentation of a child's chomp could be seen. While soothing my son, I looked over at Dillon's mommy with the expectation of a forthcoming reprimand. She asked her boy,

"Dillon, did you bite Pierce?"

"No!" Dillon protested.

But the other children gave him up.

"Ya-huh! He did it!" they exclaimed in unity, with little fingers pointing to the accused.

I surveyed the petite pack to ascertain who might be the real criminal in their midst. Their unanimity, as well as Dillon's notorious biting history, settled the question for me. It was Dillon—off with his head! Dillon's mommy must have read my mind, so she quickly interjected,

"Well, we're sorry Pierce got hurt. It really doesn't matter who did it. It just matters that Pierce is okay now."

At this, every woman there indignantly whipped her head toward Dillon's mommy, displaying an array of furrowed brows even a gallon of Botox could not smooth.

"Yes, it does matter!" I snapped. "Because if Dillon doesn't recognize biting is bad, then he won't stop doing it. And that means Pierce won't be playing with Dillon anymore!"

Some of life's most valuable lessons are learned at preschool age at a park. The lesson: Unacknowledged hurtful behavior causes division on playfields and harvest fields. Love requires accountability, and recognition of wrongdoing is essential to a sincere apology.

There have been beautiful moments where different church organizations formally recognized prejudicial practices, and even joined together in prayers and pleas of repentance. Yet, the acknowledgment did not go deep enough; it only dusted the surface of the sin. We have not gone back in a comprehensive way to deal with the depth of the inequity or the obstinate philosophies that rationalized its indulgence. Our overall ignorance of the church's racist past continues to influence present ministry policy, protocols, and structures. Worse, it continues to hinder the trust and inclusion of those who have experienced the bite of bias.

God considered the history of sin and grace so important for us to know, He supernaturally inspired 66 books detailing over 5,000 years of faith and failing. We learn in the Bible's pages of God's faithfulness to the fragile, and in so doing, find fresh faith and informed direction for the future. Likewise, we must make an unflinching observation of our past, as it gives us both assurance and admonition for our future together.

Spanish philosopher George Santayana is credited with the adage, "Those who cannot remember the past are condemned to repeat it." Dutch philosopher Baruch Spinoza put it this way: "If you want the present to be different from the past, study the past."

Though most believers are completely unaware of how deeply prejudice was embedded within the foundational movements of our faith, ministry leadership does not have the luxury of ignorance. That is, not if we truly desire to move forward into inclusive and multicultural Kingdom ministry.

HORRORS AND HEROES

Below I've given a short summary of justified and exercised racism within the policies, activities, and doctrines of the three largest Christian movements in the world today. This summary is by no means detailed or comprehensive. It is only a short synopsis, or snapshot, to punctuate the principle and encourage you in further research and study.

CATHOLICISM. From its influence on the Roman Empire to the adventures of Christopher Columbus to the Crusades and onward, the Catholic Church has advanced the message of the Cross throughout the world. Catholic heritage is crowded by multitudes of gracious, self-sacrificing, and noble saints and servants who gave their all for Christ and their fellowman. Nonetheless, its woeful history of violence, domination, corruption, and racism also cannot be ignored or excused. The abuse, enslavement, and, too often, the massacre of indigenous people groups was strongly supported by the church and embedded in its early doctrine of Christian expansionism. For example, in 1452, the *Dum Diversas* from the Pope gave the Portuguese authority to "invade, capture, vanquish, and subdue all Saracens (Arab Muslims), pagans, and other enemies of Christ, to put them into perpetual slavery, and to take away all their possessions and property." In 1493, the Inter Caetera by Pope Alexander VI asserted "the rights of Spain and Portugal to colonize, convert, and enslave. It also justifie[d] the enslavement of Africans."[1]

Other official papal letters and documents continued with similar messages. For instance, the "Doctrine of Discovery," a church teaching that "established spiritual, political, and legal justification for colonization and seizure of land not inhabited by Christians," authorized the exploitation of people groups, communities, their lands, and possessions. "This ideology supported the dehumanization of those living on the land and their dispossession, murder, and forced assimilation. The doctrine fueled white supremacy insofar as white European settlers claimed they were instruments of divine design and possessed cultural superiority," reports the Upstander Project.[2] The conquering and subjugation of non-Anglo people groups became undisputed doctrinal privilege and practice.

Though the Catholic Church and Pope Leo XIII denounced the act of slavery in 1890, it wasn't until 1965 when the church condemned it in the official church document, the *Gaudium et Spes,* The Pastoral Constitution on the Church in the Modern World. Though slavery was finally and formally denounced, full integration and leadership opportunities for people of color continue to be a challenge for the Catholic Church.[3]

PROTESTANTISM. The protest of Catholicism's materialism, corruption, and legalism was initiated by Martin Luther in 1517 with his "95 Theses." The Great Reformation, which eventually caused separation from the Catholic Church, was fueled by the truth that the Bible, not tradition, should be the sole source of spiritual authority. Martin Luther and the printing press were powerfully used by God to bring the Gospel to a wider audience of people. Yet, this reformation also had prejudice seeded into its groundwork. Frustrated by his inability to convert Jews to Christianity, in 1543, Luther published *On the Jews and Their Lies,* in which he said the Jews were a "base, whoring people." He claimed they were full of "the devil's feces . . . which they wallow in like swine." He went on to call for their harsh treatment:

> First, to set fire to their synagogues or schools. . . . This is to be done in honor of our Lord and of Christendom so that God might see that we are Christians. . . .
>
> Second, I advise that their houses also be razed and destroyed.
>
> Third, I advise that all their prayer books and *Talmudic* writings, in which such idolatry, lies, cursing, and blasphemy are taught, be taken from them.
>
> Fourth, I advise that their *rabbis* be forbidden to teach henceforth on pain of loss of life and limb. . . .
>
> Fifth, I advise that safe-conduct on the highways be abolished completely for the Jews. For they have no business in the countryside. . . .
>
> Sixth, I advise that *usury* be prohibited to them and that all cash and treasure of silver and gold be taken from them. . . .
>
> Seventh, I recommend putting a flail, an ax, a hoe, a spade, a distaff, or a spindle into the hands of young, strong Jews and Jewesses and letting them earn their bread in the sweat of their brow. . . . But if we are afraid that they might harm us or our wives, children, servants, cattle, etc., . . . then let us emulate the common sense of other nations such as France, Spain, Bohemia, etc., . . . then eject them forever from the country.

Luther added, "We are at fault in not slaying them."[4] The predominant viewpoint of most historians is that Luther's anti-Jewish rhetoric significantly contributed to anti-Semitism in Germany, and granted support for the Nazi Party's attacks on Jews. Notably, almost every anti-Jewish book printed in the Third Reich contained references to and quotations from Luther.

Yet, we can't blame only the Nazis for using Luther's words for their own devices. Sadly, the Protestant Church was a cohort in the devilish depravity. On December 17, 1941, seven Lutheran regional church confederations sided with the policy of the Nazis, forcing Jews to wear yellow badges. They stated, "since after his bitter experience Luther had [strongly] suggested preventive measures against the Jews and their expulsion from German territory." Christopher J. Probst said, "A very large number of German Protestant ministers and pastors used Luther's publications to justify the hostility of the German National Socialists against the Jewish people.[5]

Since the 1980s, most Lutheran organizations have strongly denounced and distanced themselves from Luther's writings regarding Jews. In 1982 the Lutheran World Federation issued a statement saying, "We Christians must purge ourselves of any hatred of the Jews and any sort of teaching of contempt for Judaism." Nonetheless, Luther's anti-Semitic influence in Protestantism and national politics cannot be denied. Writing in the *Lutheran Quarterly* in 1987, Dr. Johannes Wallmann stated:

> The assertion that Luther's expressions of anti-Jewish sentiment have been of major and persistent influence in the centuries after the Reformation, and that there exists a continuity between Protestant anti-Judaism and modern racially oriented anti-Semitism, is at present wide-spread in the literature; since the

Second World War it has understandably become the prevailing opinion.

In honoring Martin Luther and the Protestant Reformation, it is also critical we identify the anti-Jewish and White supremacy sentiments still being regurgitated within the dogmas and creeds of racist organizations today. In May 2022, an 18-year-old male killed ten people in a Buffalo, New York, grocery store because they were people of color and because of his belief in lies fueled by a white nationalistic zeal. And who could forget the harrowing chants of the White nationalists who defiantly marched the streets of Charlottesville, Virginia, in 2017? With fiery torches in hand and Christian crosses emblazoned on banners, they shouted, "Jews will not replace us!"

PENTECOSTALISM. The Pentecostal Movement that began on Azusa Street in Los Angeles in 1906 became one of the fastest-growing Christian movements in the world. Per the Center for the Study of Global Christianity's 2020 report, Pentecostals and Charismatics presently comprise 26 percent of all Christians worldwide, and have become the largest expression of Christianity in Latin America and the Caribbean (*Doe1.org*). The tidal wave of God's Spirit birthed at the mission on Azusa Street has washed over every nation and filled countless people with the power of Pentecost.

William Seymour, the one-eyed son of slaves, was the spark that set the Azusa Street Revival into an unquenchable blaze, leading it with gentle humility and courageous love. In its genesis, the revival valued not only the baptism in the Spirit, with the evidence of tongues, and holy lifestyles. It was also intergenerational, inter-denominational, interracial, and unbiased regarding gender. Men and women preached, prayed, and led together equally. Black people laid hands on white people without prejudice. Regardless of class, color, or creed, people fellowshiped, worshiped, knelt at the altar, ministered, and received the baptism in the Holy Spirit side by side. Even little children spoke in tongues, prophesied, and evangelized with freedom and boldness. To those at the origins of the movement, the baptism was poured out not only for the infilling but to unite the church racially before the Second Coming of Christ.

Sadly, the remarkable ethnic unity found at the beginnings of Azusa Street did not last. Years before the revival, William Seymour had humbly sat outside a classroom in Houston to listen to the lectures of a man named Charles Parham. Parham, whom some consider one of the fathers of the Pentecostal movement, taught on the baptism in the Holy Spirit and speaking in tongues, which stirred Seymour's spirit. However, Charles Parham was a well-documented racist. When Parham later heard of the outpouring of the Holy Spirit at Azusa Street, he came to Los Angeles and attempted to take leadership of the revival away from Seymour. When unsuccessful, Parham focused his energies to hijack the movement by establishing a competing congregation a few blocks from the Azusa mission, claiming to be its true leader. He worked systematically to discredit Seymour and the Biblical nature of the interracial congregation, writing and preaching White supremacist doctrine.[6]

Below are excerpts from the reflections of Charles Parham shortly after his confrontation with Seymour and the Azusa Street leadership. A warning here: These quotes are quite explicit, but I've chosen to leave them in their raw and crude form, that in wincing, we may become wiser. Parham wrote:

> I have seen meetings where all crowded together around the altar and laying across one another like

hogs, blacks, and whites mingling; this should bring a blush of shame to devils, let alone angels, and yet all this was charged to the Holy Spirit."[7]

Later, in an editorial, Parham wrote:

> Men and women, whites and blacks, knelt together or fell across one another, frequently, a white woman, perhaps of wealth and culture, could be seen thrown back in the arms of a big buck n******, and held tightly thus as she shivered and shook in freak imitation of Pentecost. Horrible, awful shame!"[8]

The revival began to splinter down racial lines under the constant barrage of Parham and other White ministers. Subsequently, the congregation at Azusa shrank in size and influence, while White congregations prospered and Pentecostal denominations formed. In 1913, the Apostolic Faith World-Wide Camp Meeting in Los Angeles was held—a gathering to celebrate and advance the Pentecostal revival. William Seymour was not even invited. Seymour ultimately lost his vision for an interracial community of faith in 1914, when White ministers left the Church of God in Christ (predominantly Black) to form the Assemblies of God. In 1915, Seymour, in his "Doctrines and Disciplines of the Azusa Street Apostolic Faith Mission," expressed his disillusionment with a multi-racial ministry, and decided to exclude white people from leading in his church.

In contemplating the history of racism in Pentecostalism, Chris Green writes:

> Parham was convinced that history proved beyond question that "certain races had more spiritual insight and ability than others," and that "in both the church and the world at large, it was thus clear that the better races were to rule and the lesser races were to follow." Therefore, it is incumbent upon white Pentecostals both to acknowledge this history in all of its

horrible detail, and to begin to make restitution for the wrongs done to their brothers and sisters.[9]

Similarly, Bishop Ithiel Clemmons exhorted, "The responsibility for promoting racial healing rests with all Americans, but especially with the church; and especially with those Christians for whom Pentecost is the metaphor that defines their vision."

This summary of historic racism in the church most likely generates conflicting emotions and thoughts. While we honor the noble but fragile vessels who served God's wondrous work, we must not ignore the horrific harm they did to countless souls and the church as a whole. It is inexcusable to make excuses for prejudiced words and actions because of the times these men lived in and the cultures they were from. They were representatives of a greater culture, a greater vision, and a greater cause; that is, God's kingdom. In moving forward, we must exercise the spiritual maturity to recognize the duplicity in many of our pioneering ministries and ministers: honoring the holiness while also calling out wickedness. We should credit the Catholic Church for its remarkable impact throughout the world. Yet, in doing so, we cannot ignore the corrupt and sometimes savage history of subjugation, violence, and corruption.

We should celebrate the courage of Martin Luther's reformation message, while forcefully rejecting his anti-Semitic rantings. Charles Parham's passion for the move of the Holy Spirit can be honored while refusing to defend the blatant and unholy spirit of racism. William Seymour should be commemorated as the father of the Pentecostal Movement, one who envisioned and founded a Spirit-filled multicultural community. Yet in doing so, we also observe that after years of enduring unrelenting brutal racist attacks, he fatigued in the fight, and bitterly abandoned the dream. Pastor and author Adina Kring makes this appeal:

> No matter how rancid the racism or wicked the attack, we can't give up on God's vision for interracial ministry! Seymour gave up his dream in the end, but we who have experienced prejudice, can't let ourselves become bitter and turn back, no matter what. We must pick up this baton and run forward with it or we'll find ourselves back where we started. As a Black female minister, trust, I know how cruel, paralyzing, and evil racism and sexism are. That is exactly why we cannot acquiesce and lose ground. We cannot allow ourselves to become discouraged, bitter, and concede God's fight. So, "Let us not be weary in well-doing; for in due season, we shall reap if we faint not" (Galatians 6:9 KJV).

The knowledge of prejudice, so deeply woven into the fabric of our faith beginnings, should profoundly move and motivate us, not discourage or defeat us. It should even provoke us to holy anger, as it did our Lord, at the Temple in Jerusalem. With whip in hand and in righteous rage, Christ drove away the money-changers, thieves, and animals that crowded out the Gentiles from His Temple courts, crying, "My house will be called a house of prayer [for all nations, Isaiah 56:7], but you are making it a den of robbers" (Matthew 21:13).

Jemar Tisby writes:

> The time for the American church's complicity in racism has long past. It is time to cancel compromise. It is time to practice courageous Christianity.... Courageous Christianity embraces racial and ethnic diversity. It stands against any person, policy, or practice that would dim the glory of God reflected in the life of human beings from every tribe and tongue.[10]

It is past time we bring the vengeance of the Lord against the racism which displaces the nations from His courts and presence.

AT MY OWN FRONT DOOR

The Pentecostal denomination which I love and am gratefully and gladly a part of has, admittedly, its own challenging history with racism. The Church of God was birthed sovereignly, by the power of the Holy Spirit, in a small group of humble Appalachian believers in 1886. Since then, we have become a mighty army for Christ in almost every nation and culture around the globe, with a constituency of more than seven million members in 180 nations and territories. Despite this powerful testimony and our great missional zeal, we have struggled through the years to uproot the toxic weed of prejudice. Though a founding leader traveled across the country to sit under the ministry of African-American pastor William Seymour of the Azusa Street Revival, the first generation of the movement remained primarily Caucasian in constituency and segregated in practice.

In the early 1900s, our first general overseer, A. J. Tomlinson, brought a more inclusive influence within the denomination. Tomlinson had grown up in a racially diverse community with a family heritage that had participated in the Underground Railroad. As overseer, he was instrumental in bringing African-Americans into the organization, credentialing them as ministers, and appointing Black overseers. He openly expressed his frustration with the challenges to racial inclusion in the South yet still agreed to separate Black and Latino ministry structures from White. Though Tomlinson believed in an inclusive theology, he operated in a Southern segregated tradition, advocating for separate schools, communities, and churches.[11]

As the decades passed, it became more obvious the challenge for racial equity in our organization was not only cultural but doctrinal as well. Church of God Historian David G. Roebuck observed:

> Emphasis on law and government along with order as an expected outcome may also have contributed to the Church of God's lack of a prophetic stand against the injustices of racism. Some in the Church of God attributed the growing unrest generated by the Civil Rights Movement to be the result of devil-inspired Communism seeking to provoke civil war. Segregation was God ordained to prevent the mixing of the races. Attempts to dismantle segregation defied God's Biblical law. Although such positions were changing by the 1960s, it appears that leaders in the Church of God believed they could not advance faster than the civil laws would allow.[12]

Dr. Roebuck's observations are revelatory. However, Lee College, the flagship institution of higher education for the Church of God, did not admit African-American students until 1966 (two years after the passage of the Civil Rights Act). The institution of a separate jurisdiction for "Colored Ministries," which was overseen by White bishops, remained well into the 1970s. The State of Florida continues to have a separate jurisdiction for Black ministries to this day. Some see it as a woeful continuation of segregation, whereas others view it as "a necessary antidote to complete subjugation" by White leadership (Roebuck). Unfortunately, a number of Church of God African-American leaders remain concerned that without a separate sphere of ministry specific for Black churches in Florida, those ministries and ministers would lose their voice, identity, cultural distinctiveness, and leadership opportunities to Whites. It is felt the Cocoa-Florida Region, as it is called, allows for Black ministries to thrive without being homogenized into White culture. More importantly, it enables Black ministers to be valued, mentored, and positioned, whereas they otherwise might be overlooked.

Latinos also have separate jurisdictions in the U.S., formed primarily because of language differences. Yet, Latino church leaders, as well as Asian, also express concern for limited opportunities in the upper echelons of denominational government and ministry offices. Their concerns are based on historical and statistical facts. More than 130 years after its birth, only one African-American man and one Latino man have served in top Executive Committee leadership of the Church of God, although Anglos are a minority in global membership. Not one person of Asian descent has held any kind of top-level leadership position in Church of God history. "Ninety percent of the employees at the Church of God International Headquarters are White and the remaining 10 percent include Hispanics and African-Americans, while more than 185 nations and 36,000 churches are served worldwide," says Dr. Fijoy Johnson in his work, "Can the Church of God Pursue Ethnic Diversity in Leadership?"[13]

The General Assembly, where the election of executive leadership is held, and the selection of board members is determined, convenes only in the United States, and requires in-person attendance for voting. This significantly encumbers ministers from different countries from participation, and therefore, representation. The frustration and disappointment voiced by a great number of significant church leaders of color, coupled with our history, are a clarion call for the Church of God to do an organizational introspection and vigorous realignment. Thankfully, our leadership in recent years has worked courageously and consistently to bring change to the bylaws, procedures, and practices, as well as initiate corporate and regional repentance and restoration.

Bishop Doyle P. Scott, director of the newly formed Intercultural Advancement Ministries for the Church of God, says,

"We are not just a cross-cultural or multicultural church, but an intercultural church—interlocking with one another. People will realize this by sight, not just sound. People will want to get involved in the Church of God when they see us demonstrating diversity.... There must be an awakening. The key is all people showing up at the throne; let's give them that opportunity."[14] Under Bishop Scott's leadership, two African-descent leadership boards have been appointed: the African-Descent Commission and the African-Descent Advisory Board. Both boards work to observe, develop, educate, and position African-Descent leadership. Presently, at the time of writing, six Black men hold the position as state overseer in the U.S. However, the states they preside over have a majority contingency of Black churches. The question has been asked, Why is it leaders of color are seen as incapable of leading those outside their own race?

We still have so much more to do to realize equal representation and opportunity on platforms, pulpits, and pews. As fellow ministers of color have told me of their appalling and inexcusable experiences with racism in our organization, I have become greatly grieved. Though some of the stories relayed to me occurred in the past, far too many experiences of racial slurs, boycotts, being overlooked for positions, and open resistance based on race have happened just in recent years. *Racism is not a distant menace; it is a close and present affliction.*

The Church of God serves as an example of the internal struggle and sluggish progress of the global church to incorporate racial inclusivity, not only in the U.S. but also in countries around the world. As with so many ministries and denominations in the world today, we are being pressed by the Holy Spirit to consider what culture will be predominant within our hallowed halls—human culture or Kingdom culture. "In today's society, minorities and different non-white ethnicities do not feel valued. These individuals want to see the church as a prime example for the secular world to follow in terms of how they should treat people of color," Dr. Fijoy Johnson challenges.[15]

Instead of being dragged by the secular world into diversity, the church should instead boldly lead the world in inclusivity, because of our devotion to Scriptural and Kingdom values. The ministers and leaders of Jesus' church are called to be thermostats, not thermometers. Our role is to set the atmosphere according to God's Word, not to merely respond and react to the world's cultural climate (principle put forth in King's *Letter From a Birmingham Jail*). The church will never be able to claim its sacred calling of racial unity and multicultural ministry if we avoid or make excuses for its marred history, complicity, and, too often, current complacency. Instead, we will continue to suffer from the pain, the pus, and the powerlessness of division. So, for the love of our God, His Word, and His people, it is time for the Church to engage in holy lament that we may move forward as one fully reconciled and united people.

THE R'S HAVE IT

There are no fancy formulas available for rooting out prejudice, ending the sin cycle, and initiating racial reconciliation. Yet, there are simple sequential principles, that can lead us through the process to the realization of Jesus' dream church. I call them the "R's of Reconciliation."

First, we must *recognize* the sin and injustice of prejudice, along with the pain it has caused. It is essential our observation of racism is viewed beyond the historical, overt, and blatant, but also acknowledges its reality in the present—covert and systemic. Jemar Tisby says,

> History and Scripture teach us that there can be no reconciliation without repentance. There can be no repentance without confession. And there can be no confession without truth . . . telling the truth so that reconciliation—robust, consistent, honest reconciliation—might occur across racial lines.[16]

The humble work of recognizing and telling the whole truth regarding injustice is essential to moving forward together.

Second, ***repent*** of the sin of racism wholeheartedly, without excuse or justification. Repentance is not just feeling sorry that something hurtful happened. The Apostle Paul wrote in 2 Corinthians 7:9-10:

> Yet now I am happy, not because you were made sorry, but because your sorrow led you to repentance. . . . Godly sorrow brings repentance that leads to salvation and leaves no regret, but worldly sorrow brings death (ESV).

For too long we've said our "sorrys" to people of color, without corresponding action to remedy what caused the wound. What we need is not shallow sorrys, but authentic godly grief leading to repentance. *Repentance* literally means to "turn around and go the other way." True repentance always motivates action. In some situations, the sin of racism was committed by another generation. Yet, we can promote healing through "representational" repentance for sins committed nationally, regionally, ethnically, or by previous family members. This is not some spooky prayer for the dead, or a pious attempt of substitution to absolve others. Let me state emphatically: Only Jesus is our sin substitute. Representational repentance occurs when the present generation identifies, acknowledges, and repents for the sins of their own people, resolving the sin legacy stops with them.

Third, **respect** the individual or people group victimized by the sin of racism. Respect means to honor and validate the inherent dignity, uniqueness, worth, wisdom, and grace within a person or people group. Prejudice becomes a stronghold when people are demoted and downgraded from their actual value. Racism and sexism are the results of a mindset of the superiority of one group over another. Respecting someone involves observing their value and equality, honoring cultural distinctives, (history, language, art, titles, perspectives), and their strengths. It also means making room for their voice to be heard, and attributing worth to unique and valuable perspectives.

Fourth, **reconcile.** The definition of *reconciliation* is "to make amends." It also means to make things compatible or consistent with each other. For instance, when we reconcile our finances, we account for what has been debited and deposited. Relational reconciliation involves equalizing the relationship, making deposits, creating partnerships, and forging a purposed future together.

GIANTS AND GIANT KILLERS

When it comes to racism, the church has been unable to get the traction that moves us forward in a meaningful way. Bluntly, we seem to be repeatedly engaged in backyard skirmishes but never win the war. I believe that is because we haven't truly dealt with, past the point of apologies, the historic devils that thwart our present efforts. Unreconciled and unrepented past sin continues to have authority and influence in the present.

When Israel failed to eradicate the Philistines upon entrance to their Promised Land, God instructed Joshua's army to annihilate the Philistine people, killing even the women and children. God's command to destroy even the infant Philistines seems extreme.

Let's Kill This Giant

Yet, baby Philistines grow up into giant Philistines, just as baby sins mature into giant threats. Young David should have never had to deal with the colossus Philistine named Goliath. Because his predecessors failed to swing the sword, Israel struggled with constant encroachment on God's sovereign land. (See 1 Samuel 17.) The church's relentless fight with racism, classism, misogyny, and bias is evidence, the seemingly harmless baby devil of prejudice was not put to the sword properly in previous generations. For this giant now contends for our last-days harvest field as a roaring ogre. I am of the generation that has valued caution, grace, and process over justice and equity. Dr. Martin Luther King penned from the Birmingham jail in 1963, "I felt that the white ministers, priests, and rabbis of the South would be some of our strong allies. Instead . . . all too many others have been more cautious than courageous and have remained silent behind the anesthetizing security of stained-glass windows."[17]

Six decades later, our desire to be gracious, careful, and not offensive, has allowed the devil of racism to dominate another generation. To quote Estrelda Alexander, president of the William Joseph Seymour Foundation, "Sometimes you have to disturb the peace to preserve the unity." We have sinned in not dealing scrupulously, rigorously, and methodically with it. For, if we had, our youth would not be battling over a segregated church, wounded people, and worldwide cynicism over our hypocrisy. *We were called to kill this giant.* We must repent for not putting it to the sword—every little cooing giant and our precious coddled cultural sins.

For in this day, God is raising a generation of Davids around the world! Dressed in simple shepherd's clothing, and armed with the Spirit, they will not coddle or coo at cute cultural traditions, mindsets, or administrations that give even an inch of ground to prejudice. Like David, who wouldn't give even one shabby sheep to a bear, they will not concede a centimeter of God's promised territory, one heart redeemed by Christ, or one culture called to sing His praise. They will be ruthless and pitiless with this sin. Without hesitation, they will ensure not one cancerous cell of prejudice survives in the hearts, homes, churches, and administrative structures of Christ's glorious church. Zealous for God, passionate for His people, and loving the lost, they will run toward the giant of racism, declaring, "I come against you in the name of the Lord Almighty . . . whom you have defied. This day the Lord will deliver you into my hands, and I'll strike you down and cut off your head" (1 Samuel 17:45-46).

Endnotes

1. *www.nlm.nih.gov>timeline*
2. *www.upstanderproject.org/firstlight/doctrine*
3. Patrick Saint-Jean, S.J. scatholic.org/articles/202009/we-need-to-talk-about-racism-in-the-catholic-church/
4. *Jewishvirtuallibrary.org*
5. Christopher J. Probst, *Demonizing the Jews: Luther and the Protestant Church in Nazi Germany* (Indiana University Press, 2012)
6. Allan Anderson, "The Dubious Legacy of Charles Parham: Racism and Cultural Insensitivities among Pentecostals," *Pneuma* 27, no. 1 (Spring 2005)
7. Charles Parham, *The Everlasting Gospel* (Apostolic Faith Bible College, 1911)
8. *The Apostolic Faith* (April 3, 1925)
9. Chris Green, *The Spirit that Makes Us (Number) One*
10. Jemar Tisby, *The Color of Compromise.*
11. *Like A Mighty Army* Pathway Press, 2008
12. "Unraveling the Cords that Divide: Cultural Challenges and Race Relations in the Church of God (Cleveland, Tennessee)," presented at the 40th Annual Meeting of the Society for Pentecostal Studies
13. Fijoy Johnson, *Can the Church of God Pursue Ethnic Diversity in Leadership?* Bethel University, 2019
14. "Multicultural Togetherness" by Lance Colkmire, interview of Doyle P. Scott (*Church of God Evangel* January/February 2022)
15. Fijoy Johnson, *Ethnic Diversity in Leadership*
16. Jemar Tisby, *The Color of Compromise*
17. Martin Luther King Jr., "The Negro Is Your Brother," *The Atlantic Monthly* (August 1963)

7

Prayers of a Dying Man

We huddled close to him to hear every lingering whisper. My grandfather was a giant in faith and had lived a lifetime of adventure with Jesus. Now in his mid-90s, his big brave heart was beating out its closing drumbeats. For a man who had been larger than life to us, his frame appeared small and fragile as he lay almost motionless in the bed. His breath became slow and rattled. Hushed voices and muffled weeping could be heard behind me as I knelt beside the bed and cradled his precious wrinkled hand in mine.

The hours passed and the family briefly exited the room to discuss final plans together in the hallway. Left alone to share a last moment with him, I tearfully whispered, "Thank you, Grandpa! Thank you for living a life of authentic faith and courageous love."

Suddenly, I was aware he was looking straight at me. He'd been unconscious all day and not expected to revive, so I was startled.

"Grandpa!" I cried out.

In a weak raspy voice, he asked the same question every time he saw me: "Are you preachin' preachin'?"

This time, however, it was more a directive than a question. He reached out his feeble hand and laid it atop my head. I didn't hear him pray a word, but I could feel the power of his impartation and blessing. He passed into glory soon after. Though committed to my call to preach before this patriarchal commission, the prayers of my dying grandfather amplified my assignment and quickened my pace. I haven't stopped "preachin' preachin'" since. That is how precious, persuasive, and powerful the final words of a dying man are. They relay the essence of his heart and soul; his highest hopes and utmost longing.

Most scholars believe Christ's final words and prayers, prior to Gethsemane and the Cross, are found in John 14 through 17. Here, Christ prays not that His followers would be authoritative or gifted. He pleads that we would love each other and become "one":

> "My prayer is not for them alone. I pray also for those who will believe in me through their message, that all of them may be one, Father, just as you are in me and I am in you. May they also be in us so that the world may believe that you have sent me. I have given them the glory that you gave me, that they may be one as we are one—I in them and you in me—so that they may be brought to complete unity. Then the world will know that you sent me and have loved them even as you have loved me" (17:20-23).

We, God's people, are being challenged by Christ's dying prayer in these tumultuous days. Defying the carnal propensity to divide according to color, class, politics, or liturgy, we're being called by Jesus himself to "oneness." Jesus' dying prayer drew a vivid portrait of His dream church:

- A church around the world so united, we mirror the oneness of the Holy Trinity: "I pray . . . that all of them may be one, Father, just as you are in me and I am in you" (John 17:21).

- His called ones utilizing the glory and power of the Holy Spirit to seal its bonds of unity, not to advance separate and segregated missions: "I have given them the glory that you gave me, that they may be one as we are one" (v. 22).

- A holy community moving in such sync, agreement, and united purpose, we reveal the validity of Christ's love for the world: "Then the world will know that you sent me and have loved them even as you have loved me" (v. 23).

POSSIBLE IMPOSSIBILITIES

Would Jesus pray for something unattainable for us? Of course not! Christ wasn't asking for a pie-in-the-sky notion or a fuzzy, esoteric, after-earth future. He was praying for what is possible here and now, with His help. Though unity among God's people may seem to be unpractical, unfeasible, and impossible, the Bible we believe and preach tells us repeatedly to have faith for what seems impossible:

God declared to Abraham regarding Sarah's impending pregnancy in Genesis 18:14, "Is anything too hard for the Lord?"

The prophet Jeremiah declared in Jeremiah 32:17, "Nothing is too hard for you."

The Lord responded to Jeremiah, "I am the Lord, the God of all mankind. Is anything too hard for me?" (v. 27).

In Luke 1:37, the angel reminded Mary, "For with God nothing shall be impossible" (KJV).

Jesus challenged the father of a demon-possessed son, saying, "Everything is possible for one who believes" (Mark 9:23). In Matthew 19:26, Jesus told His disciples, "With man this is impossible, but with God all things are possible."

In Luke 18:27, "Jesus replied, 'What is impossible with man is possible with God.'"

We quote these powerful verses when believing for healing, deliverance, salvation, forgiveness, provision, and evangelistic endeavors. So why shouldn't we claim the same for Jesus' fervent dying prayer for unity in His church? Shouldn't we consider Jesus' prayer our assignment as much as we do His commission to spread the Good News? The unity of a small group of praying believers in the Upper Room provoked wind, fire, and the infilling of the Holy Spirit in Acts 2. The church was birthed, and 3,000 people were saved. What would happen if millions of believers today were determined to walk in unity regardless of color, culture, class, or liturgical expression? It's an awe-inspiring contemplation, already envisioned in Jesus' powerful prayer. All it requires is that we say "yes" to God and offer ourselves as His dream partners.

DREAM OR NIGHTMARE?

The late Archbishop Desmond Tutu said, "God's dream is that you and I and all of us will realize that we are family, that we are made for togetherness, for goodness, and for compassion." Perhaps we've been tempted to give up on Jesus' dream because we don't understand what unity or oneness looks or sounds like. We perceive a unified church as some undefinable amoeba, where function, characteristics, and forward motion is indiscernible.

I was just a kid during the hippie movement of the 1960s and '70s. Reacting to the hypocrisy and materialism of culture, the hippies checked out of society altogether. Filling the streets and parks with guitar-strumming poets, psychedelics, and free love, they hoped to change and unify the world. John Lennon captured their imagination with his song, "Imagine" in which he envisioned there being no Heaven, no hell, no religion, no countries. Most of these hopeful, long-haired, bell-bottomed kids' vision of unity simply meant listening to cool music together, wearing the same groovy clothes, and sharing a great high.

The "oneness" John Lennon imagined, however, entailed the dismantling of spiritual truths, the destruction of national and cultural borders, and the redistribution of wealth. From his Manhattan penthouse, Lennon crooned that it would somehow miraculously create a "brotherhood of man." Rather than a lovely dream, it resembled more of a nightmare: communism rather than community. Obviously, that was not the kind of "oneness" Jesus was praying for. His prayer envisioned nations of people, with diverse customs and cultures, freely joined together in a Kingdom community. People allied not by sameness, but by a heavenly faith identity and missional purpose.

EBONY AND IVORY

"Well, you two are just a party in a box, aren't you?" the flight attendant chuckled.

"I want what you two are drinking!" the lady in the seat next to us said.

"It's just Coke!" we exclaimed in unison. I'd been laughing so hard, tears were streaming down my face and messing up my mascara. I tried to catch my breath and pull myself together before the plane landed. We'd soon meet the bishop, and I needed to appear more dignified.

It was always this way with my friend Adina. Once my disciple, now my best friend, she had wandered into the church right off the street and fell "hard" in love with Jesus. Miraculously transformed by grace, she approached me a few months later wanting to be mentored, so I took her under my wing. I believe in on-the-go mentoring. This means "Come help me, and I'll teach you as we go." She would come to my office daily after her work and do anything I asked, from filing to cleaning, and even shuttling my kids around. Never have I witnessed a more dedicated, people-loving, loyal, and hard-working soul than she. Adina soon became indispensable to me, so I formally made her my administrative assistant. As the years passed, we became forged together as friends. We couldn't be more different in background, personality, or race. She is tall, slim, outgoing, beautiful, and Black. I am short, blond, introverted, frequently grumpy, and White. Nonetheless, we are sister-soldiers, ebony and ivory, coffee and cream. One of our greatest joys was to travel together when I was asked to preach for conferences.

On this particular trip, we were headed to the Deep South, where I would be ministering at a regional camp meeting, and then in local churches on the weekend. Adina had originally come from New York and relocated to Arizona. She had never been to the South and was looking forward to the experience. Met at the airport by the welcoming smiles of the state bishop and his wife, our luggage was quickly loaded into their SUV, and we started on the long drive to the campground. Coming from dry, dusty, and brown, Arizona, the lush green countryside was intoxicating. Seated comfortably in the cushy back passenger seats, we rolled down our windows to enjoy the moist warm air.

The sun began to set, and our hosts stopped at a quaint country restaurant along the side of the road. Upon our entrance, every person turned around and stared, and whispered curiously as the hostess took us to our table. After ordering traditional southern food, Adina and I excused ourselves to wash our hands, again sensing the eyes of the customers and servers upon us. While there, Adina started up an animated conversation with a young girl. Adina is annoyingly friendly. She'll know the birthday, anniversary, height, and weight of everyone in line for a hamburger at McDonald's before it's her turn to order. I left Adina with her new friend and returned to the table. Five minutes later, a large white woman bolted out of the restroom door, dragging the girl by the arm. Adina followed cautiously behind.

"But she's my friend, Mommy!" the girl protested loudly. "She's not your friend! She's a n******! Don't you ever talk to a n****** again! You hear me?" the woman shrieked.

Our hosts were horrified and apologetic. Adina and I were both dumbfounded. She had experienced racism all her life, but never as raw and rabid as this. To Adina's credit and courage, she shook the hatefulness off as we headed back on the road. By this time the sun had dipped into the trees and the headlights of the SUV were all that illuminated our passage onward. As he drove, the bishop spoke into our quiet contemplations:

"Miss Adina and Pastor Rae, once again, I'm really sorry about what happened back there. You're in the Deep South now. There are lots of people here who are still caught in the web of racism. You may experience it from some of the people at the camp meeting—maybe even from some of the pastors, unfortunately. You're being stared at because it is unusual for Whites and Blacks to be such close friends."

His wife interjected, "That's why we've been so excited to have you come. We saw you minister together in Tennessee.

We knew right away we wanted you to come here. We've been fastin' and prayin' for this time. We're askin' God for a breakthrough."

The bishop looked up into the rearview mirror as he drove, and caught my eye, then continued, "Pastor Rae, we are giving you absolute freedom to minister as the Lord leads you."

"I'm humbled by your trust, Bishop," I answered. "You are a very brave man!" We all laughed together.

An hour later, we turned onto a dirt road and up to a large lodge. Using the headlights of the SUV to illuminate the front porch, our host fumbled with the keys to the door while Adina and I looked nervously into the dark woods surrounding us. Not a single light from a house or campfire could be seen. Adina's concern was obvious as our suitcases were placed in separate suites: mine at one end of the lodge and hers at the other. Adina asked our hosts, "Where are we? Is there anyone else coming?"

"You're on the campground in the speaker's lodge, darlin'," the bishop's wife answered. "You get the place to yourself tonight. Others will be comin' round tomorrow. We'll be here early in the mornin' to take you to breakfast. Good night, sleep tight!"

Then they left. I was delighted to have the big room to myself and appreciative for the quiet before the start of the conference. Adina, however, was preoccupied and pensive. We went to our respective suites, and I began to unpack my suitcase. Moments later, I heard a strong knock at the door. Adina stood there with suitcase in hand.

"I'm not sleeping down there by myself!" she stated firmly, not waiting for my invitation.

"Okay, it'll be a pajama party, then! There are two beds in here anyway," I observed, and then waved her in.

She immediately went from one window to the next, looking intently into the dark woods for any movement.

"What are you looking for?" I questioned. "Burning crosses."

"Adina!"

"Oh, my Lord! Look! There's one!" she gasped in horror, as I ran to the window. Nothing out there but darkness. She howled with laughter.

"That's not funny!" I grumbled. Then we both fell silent, reflecting on the evening's events.

"I'm so sorry, Friend," I whispered. It was so inadequate.

I turned away so she wouldn't see the tears welling up in my eyes.

What did I bring my friend into? I thought. *I'm so naïve, sometimes.*

Adina sensed my struggle.

"Pastor Friend," she said softly, "I knew what I might be getting into when I said I'd come with you here. I'm not afraid, because God is going to do something with us that will change the spiritual and physical complexion of this region. I know that sounds arrogant, but we are here on divine assignment."

When we entered the back of the meeting hall the next night, we noticed among the nearly two thousand in attendance, the majority were Anglos. A small group of African-Americans sat at the back together. An even smaller group of Latinos sat to the side with earphones for translation on their heads. There was no mingling between the three groups. As we followed the bishop to the front, eager anticipation welled up in some people, while hot contempt steamed out of others. Instead of irritation, I felt tremendous compassion for the latter group. Caught in the vice grip of deceit, hate had hardened their hearts and darkened their minds. They were trapped, but Jesus would free them.

The anointing on the messages I brought at the conference had a prophetic penetration I had never experienced before. Adina joined me nightly on the platform to share words of wisdom and discernment that were life-changing to countless individuals. I intentionally kept her close by my side at the altars as the Holy Spirit moved through us together in signs, wonders, healing, and deliverance. At first, some white folk recoiled when Adina stretched out her hand to touch them. Yet, when the power of God began to flow through her, their prejudice melted away, and their hunger superseded their racist reservations. Those who were once cold and withdrawn became eager and hopeful. As I preached, I intentionally would leave the platform and walk down the aisle toward the groups in the back, placing my hand on their shoulders in affirmation.

Curious eyes followed us after the services, watching how we related to each other—observing the ease, mutual respect, and natural servanthood between friends. Many pastors and leaders eagerly gathered over meals to talk with us about how to break down racial walls and forge Kingdom partnerships. As the conference progressed, the leadership tables became more racially blended and comfortable. There were a few, of course, who kept their distance, judging with narrowed eyes and pursed lips. We ignored them.

Early Sunday morning, we drove with a local pastor further down the wooded road to his church. A gentleman with quiet strength, he explained to us the church he led was multicultural, the first of its kind in these parts. The pastor and his family had experienced threats and intense persecution. Old traditional prejudices still held ground in this county. Not until that very year had community and school events become integrated. Living in the West, I'd assumed such things were in the distant past. I was immediately intimidated; Adina was not. Her strength, dignity, and grace to refuse offense bolstered my courage. God showed up in that Sunday service. Souls were saved, bodies healed, and the stronghold of prejudice broken. Not because of Adina and me, but because a humble but determined servant-hearted pastor had courageously prayed, prepared, and planned for this miraculous moment. We ministered together alongside the pastor and his wife: ebony and ivory in Kingdom partnership, releasing an exponential anointing and grace.

Our plane ride home was unusually quiet for Adina and me. Occasionally, we would glance at each other, reach out for each other's hands, and let the tears stream down our faces. No words were necessary. God had done beyond what could be verbalized. He had used a courageous bishop, a determined pastor, and two women—one black and one white—to reveal His grace, transform lives, and model the potential and power of multiethnic *oneness*.

UNI-VERSITY

So, what then is *oneness*? It is defined as "the state of being unified or whole, though being comprised of two or more parts; identity or harmony with someone or something."

Awestruck by its grounds, buildings, frat houses, stadiums, and long green mall, the University of Arizona, in my hometown of Tucson, conjured up hopeful college dreams for me. Attending a concert in the UofA Music Hall as a child with my parents, I asked my father what *university* meant. His answer was memorable:

> A university is where many different schools of learning, or colleges, converge together. You can study just about anything here: art, medicine, music, or engineering. *Uni-versity* means "unified diversity."

The church is called to "unified diversity." Though comprised of different colors, characteristics, backgrounds, focuses, experiences, and cultures, true oneness occurs when we choose to rally around the central person of Jesus Christ. "Uni-versity" in the church happens when we identify not according to our specific "college" of study, liturgy, and association, but rather, according to our mutual faith in Christ.

YOU'RE MUSIC TO MY EYES

In its essence, unity doesn't mean sameness. As with harmony, unity doesn't occur when everyone sounds the same—that's unison.

"Live in harmony with one another" (Romans 12:16), the Apostle Paul entreated. Harmony happens as differing tones sound out in complement of each other, making a rich chord that enhances the melody line. Each tone must be allowed to sound in its unique pitch and character for the chord to have an impact. True unity occurs when individuals, as well as people groups, are allowed to resonate, with unmuted voice, in the symphony of God's chorus.

Oneness doesn't mean being color blind either. In 1992, the girl group En Vogue recorded the funkadelic tune, "Free Your Mind," singing, "Be color-blind, don't be so shallow." So now, with the best intentions, people still echo the phrase, "I'm color-blind." Well-meaning as this statement seems, not observing the whole identity of a person, which includes their skin color, precludes the ability to truly honor ancestry, cultural heritage, and personal journey. Trillia Newbell said, "Don't be color-blind. Be color-wise."[1]

To be *color-wise* is to recognize and appreciate the unique history, tragedies, and triumphs of a person of color. If you flip to the back of this book, you'll see I am a white-skinned woman. Even so, my life has been lavishly blessed with home-grown and faith-grown children of color, as well as many deep friendships and ministry relationships with people of differing ethnicities. Despite my associations, however, I have not personally experienced the struggle and indignity of racism my children, friends, and peers encounter regularly. My whiteness precludes me from fully knowing and understanding it. That is because my skin color grants access, privilege, and safety that people of color do not possess as automatically as I do. I can't "know" the burden and trauma that comes with more melanin, but I can become color-wise. I can see, recognize, and appreciate the individual, the culture, and the character. They are music to God's eyes.

I SEE YOU

Being color-wise also means looking beyond the skin tone. When at the well in Samaria in John 4, Jesus revealed a keen cultural competency as He spoke to the Samaritan woman. Christ was not only on-point prophetically; He was well-versed culturally and philosophically. He understood the Samaritans' mindset, emotional wounding, and belief systems. Therefore, He was aware of the historical, societal, and personal significance His words and actions would have on the woman and her community. He drank from her cultural cup and then offered her the cup of His grace. Because of His cultural awareness, the entire community welcomed a Jewish Rabbi as their own Messiah into their midst. When His disciples finally joined Him, He urged them, "Open your eyes and look at the fields! They are ripe for harvest" (John 4:35). For they had been color-blind and tone-deaf to the richness, depth, and delicate intricacies of the beautiful and complicated Samaritan people.

Oneness obliges us to recognize and celebrate color as well as cultural distinctives; to look with love upon each tone and texture; to hear the rich resonance of heritage and listen to its songs of sorrows. Oneness compels us to honor inherent strengths, so we may collaborate, linking arms to expand the kingdom of God.

YES: WE CAN, WE MUST, WE WILL

"No, you can't go to your friend's house in the morning. It's MLK Day, and we're going to the march and then hangin' out at the park for the rally. Your friend can join us, but you're going with me," I insisted as my middle-school-age son rolled his eyes.

We attempted to participate in at least one community event on the Martin Luther King Jr. holiday weekend. Honoring the life and legacy of the man who gave his life fighting for freedom and equality was a value I wanted to be instilled in my children. Joining several pastor friends and members of my church, we marched together, singing, laughing, and prodding on our complaining children. The march ended at the park around the bandshell, where artists played music and speeches were made. We all enjoyed sampling the soul food and tacos. In Arizona, tacos show up everywhere!

Suddenly, across the grass amphitheater, a small group of White supremacist protestors began to press toward the seated

Prayers of a Dying Man

crowd. Young men jumped up to meet them in open confrontation. The speaker at the bandshell podium attempted to calm the scuffle, but only when senior men and women of influence rose to bring correction, did the inflamed situation finally cool. My friends and I calmed our frightened children and assured them we were safe. However, the tone of the speakers on stage changed dramatically. Justified anger shifted into hate-filled profanity.

"Pastor, let's go," insisted my friends, Pastors Jesse and Chauntel. So, we quickly gathered up our belongings and left. We drove home in silence, mulling over our disappointment, the children exhausted and asleep in the back of the van.

Finally, Chauntel, a brilliant woman and a pastor's wife in the city, broke the silence: "Wouldn't it be wonderful to be able to celebrate this weekend around Jesus and His freedom for all people? That was really Dr. King's message," she reflected longingly. Her husband nodded in agreement as he drove.

I turned and stared for a moment at her beautiful face, watching her chew her lip in frustration. Then a radical and revolutionary thought exploded in my mind.

"We should do it!" I exclaimed. "What if we held an event every year on this weekend that didn't compete with the community events, but did exactly what you just said—celebrated diversity and honored culture, with Jesus as the rally point?"

Visions were bursting in my head faster than I could relay.

"What if we invited all the different churches of every ethnicity to participate, as well as special musical and dance groups to perform?" I continued, now talking faster with excitement.

"You know how we always meet at my house during this weekend to share soul food and country cooking? What if we

137

built on that and invited all the different cultures to serve and sell food for people to sample? Would you and your church be willing to partner in something like that?"

"Yes! Yes, we can! We must! We will!" she exclaimed. We both then looked at Jesse for confirmation.

"Yes. We can, we must, and we *will*!" he said resolutely.

Freedom Festival was conceived at that moment. With a small group of our own church leaders and a few gutsy city pastors, we launched an evening of praise and celebration on Martin Luther King Holiday Weekend. It grew every year to eventually draw thousands. We invited participation and partnership from not only the African-American and Latino communities but also other more marginalized groups. People groups such as the Polynesian, Asian, East Indian, Caribbean, Arabic, and African refugee communities, to name a few. In fact, we found the African refugees and Asian churches were the most eager to make the vision a reality. Having been left out of most of the large church conferences and city endeavors, they were blessed to be partners in this project, laboring tirelessly to make it happen. As I stressed over it all coming together one year, a wise African elder said to me, "Don't worry, Pastor! An old Ethiopian proverb says, 'When spiders unite, they can tie down a lion.' We will tie down this lion."

So we did! There were Polynesian boat dances, Black gospel choirs, Mexican mariachis, Irish step dancers, Japanese sword performances, Russian violinists, country-western crooners, and African drums. Thankfully, no one ever got sick from the Mexican tamales, Southern-style collard greens, Nigerian puff-puffs, Irish stew, Puerto Rican pork, or the most dangerous of all, American hot dogs! Jesus was the center of the celebration.

He is our ultimate liberator. The Cross is the definitive equalizer. His love is our motivator and unifier.

The event became a catalyst, prompting meaningful conversations around the table between people groups and community leaders. These conversations led to the building of trusted relationships, which in turn produced fruitful Kingdom partnerships. Ministers who had once not believed in women preachers or pastors became some of my strongest allies. Many cohorts were not and are not Spirit-filled tongue-talkers like me. Yet, we discovered an ability to respect our respective differences and rally solely around Christ. Unified diversity—music to God's ears and eyes.

"How good and pleasant it is when God's people live together in unity! It is like precious oil poured on the head, running down on the beard, running down on Aaron's beard, down on the collar of his robe. It is as if the dew of Hermon were falling on Mount Zion. For there the Lord bestows his blessing, even life forevermore" (Psalm 133:1-3).

CRUCIAL THINGS

President George H. W. Bush said in his inaugural address, "In crucial things, unity. In important things, diversity. In all things, generosity." The "crucial thing" that unifies the church is our faith in Jesus Christ. It is the rally point of our cause and the shared DNA of our brotherhood. Everything else is secondary, be it doctrinal positioning or liturgical custom, and should compel generosity of grace and accommodation of expression.

Sadly, we as the church have allowed these secondary issues to divide and separate us, making the secondary things the "crucial things." Cross-cultural church unity cannot occur if we individually, denominationally, and organizationally gather around anything other than the person of Christ. Our one identity marker as a Christian is in the mark of Jesus' blood upon our hearts.

Dr. Tony Evans said:

> "God's kingdom is bigger than our disagreements. Embrace each other even when we don't do things the same. Our commitment to each other is more important than the political, cultural, or social experiences that would keep us apart. Regardless of the differences between members of the body of Christ, we are to accept one another just as God in Christ has accepted us."[2]

Oneness does not happen automatically or spontaneously. It is a decision first of the Spirit, and then of the will. It is an intentional choice to defy the flesh that supposes superiority, craves dominance, and excuses independence. The Word of God makes its appeal:

> *1 Corinthians 1:10*—I appeal to you, brothers and sisters, in the name of our Lord Jesus Christ, that all of you agree with one another in what you say and that there be no divisions among you, but that you be perfectly united in mind and thought.
>
> *Philippians 2:2*—Then make my joy complete by being like-minded, having the same love, being one in spirit and of one mind.
>
> *Ephesians 4:2-6*—Be completely humble and gentle; be patient, bearing with one another in love. Make every effort to keep the unity of the Spirit through the bond of peace. There is one body and one Spirit, just as you were called to one hope when you were called; one Lord, one faith, one baptism; one God and Father of all, who is over all and through all and in all.

Jesus made a heavenly petition that the celestial value of oneness would invade and overrule our earthly proclivity for independence through the power of His Spirit. He prayed we would be so yielded to the character of the Spirit of God that unity would be dominant in our hearts. Our will must align with the will of God. Our individual and organizational dreams must surrender to Christ's larger and vaster dream. Our pride, personal agendas, and dogmas must bow to embrace Christ's corporate vision of oneness. Yet, as with all prayer, for Christ's petition to be realized, we must determine to do our part in the partnership. Australian-American actor, musician, and activist Theodore Bikel said, "No doubt, unity is something to be desired, to be striven for, but it cannot be willed by mere declarations." We are His feet on the earth, and we must take the first steps. We must dare to do the natural, and then God will do the supernatural.

Paul's word to the Colossian believers resonates today:

> Therefore, as God's chosen people, holy and dearly loved, clothe yourselves with compassion, kindness, humility, gentleness, and patience. Bear with each other and forgive one another if any of you has a grievance against someone. Forgive as the Lord forgave you. And over all these virtues put on love, which binds them all together in perfect unity (Colossians 3:12-14).

Endnotes

1 Trillia Newbell, *United: Captured by God's Vision for Diversity*
2 *The Urban Alternative* blog, 12/14/20

III. THE MISSION

*An important assignment in a foreign land;
a strongly felt aim, ambition or calling.*

8

'We' Starts With 'Me'

Despite the stifling summer heat, the little white church on Farwell Street was packed with people. It was the late summer of 1970. Men in suits and ties, with wives in neatly pressed dresses and heels, stood worshipping next to young, stringy-haired hippies wearing hip-huggers, macrame' headbands, and platform shoes. Diverse in age, opinion, and appearance, they all stood side-by-side with hands lifted and voices raised.

"Great is Thy faithfulness, great is Thy faithfulness! Morning by morning, new mercies I see!" My squeaky 7-year-old voice soared exuberantly above the others as loudly as my lungs could emote. My mother looked down at me giggling with a mixture of embarrassment and amusement. As the pastor's daughter, I had already been in church with my parents most of the day. Despite this, I felt great anticipation something wonderful was about to happen.

My father stepped onto the small, creaky platform, moving behind the wooden pulpit. He opened his Bible to the Book of Acts, smoothing the pages flat before beginning to teach. With his unique preaching style, uncommon in those days, he never raised his voice, told jokes, or used the characteristic dramatics of most preachers. He just opened his Bible and quietly began to teach. Everyone settled down into their chairs to listen. He read passages from the first and second chapters, explaining how the disciples waited and prayed to receive the Holy Spirit promised by Jesus prior to His ascension. He described how a rushing wind filled the room, and flames of fire appeared over their heads. Then each one was filled with the Holy Spirit and spoke in other tongues. Men, women, young and old—all received. I reasoned with the pure simple faith of a child, well that means I can too!

So, I fixed my eyes on my father, concentrating on every word. Normally, like most children in long church services, boredom set in within the first moments of the sermon. Then wiggling, counting lights (I knew exactly how many were on the ceiling), pinching and provoking my brother, or drawing cartoons of pulpit preachers commenced. But not on this night! Leaning forward in my chair, I absorbed the message, as though into my soul. The invitation came for a response, and I found myself at the steps of the platform we called our altar, along with dozens of others. On my knees with my head bowed low to the ground, I could hear sobbing, whispered prayers, and then shouts of joy as people experienced their own encounter with the Holy Spirit.

"Oh, Jesus, fill me too!" I cried.

Suddenly an overwhelming sense of His presence came over me, like a warm and weighty blanket falling upon my tiny shoulders. Unimaginable joy and peace filled my heart. My face began to flush and my heart raced as my childish vocabulary transformed into the language of Heaven. Time stopped! Then I heard a sound I will never forget. I heard the audible voice of the Lord—deep, strong, and undeniable, rumbling in the depths of my spirit.

"I'm calling you to preach," He said.

"Oh yes, Lord! I say yes to You. I will always say yes to You!"

Since that memorable night on Farwell Street, the call of God has burned like an unquenchable fire within. My father, brought up in a traditional Pentecostal Holiness and patriarchal tradition, was not thrilled at my enthusiastic announcement of being called by God to preach and pastor.

"Oh, dear girl," he said later that same evening, "that can't be God. Girls are not called to preach or lead. But, how about you learn to play the piano for services?"

Realizing my father's pulpit would not be offered up to a 7-year-old girl at any time soon, I determined to start preaching at school that very week. I took advantage of recess and lunchtime to evangelize my classmates, much to the chagrin of the teachers and school principal. Because of lunchtime campaigns, my long-suffering parents received many calls from spiritually hungry parents, as well as from exasperated school officials. For the latter, I proved to be quite an irritating pint-sized zealot.

As the years went by, the determination to say yes to God in all things, and in all ways, opened many doors of opportunity. First, I served with all my heart in the more accepted places for women to minister in the church. I learned the piano and played in services, conducted the choir, served in children's ministry, hospitality, secretarial work, and, of course, led girls and women's ministries. In each of these more conventional places of female service, the favor and anointing of the Lord graciously blessed with fruitfulness. Young and old, and men and women alike were saved, healed, delivered, and filled with the Holy

Spirit. Doors began to open to people groups and places others were not so eager to go and serve: small, out-of-the-way, Black and Latino churches; juvenile-detention centers, prisons, homeless shelters, orphanages, and backwoods mission trips.

"You can't go there—you can't do that! You're just a girl," many said.

"I am. But I'm a girl who has said yes to a great big God," I would respond.

God finds pure delight in pouring His uncommon grace into the most common of vessels. He loves to do the extraordinary in what the world views as ordinary, the supernatural through the natural, and the miraculous in the mundane. Pastor Michael Todd said, "Limitations are an invitation for God's glory." Paul eloquently addressed this astounding truth in 1 Corinthians 1:27-29 when he stated:

> But God has chosen the foolish things of the world to put to shame the wise; God chose the weak things of the world to put to shame the strong. God chose the lowly things of this world and the despised things – and the things that are not – to nullify the things that are, so that no one may boast before him (NKJV).

JUST SAY YES!

God chose Jacob—a conniving, cheating momma's boy—to bear the name of His chosen people Israel and to be its patriarch. God selected Moses, a stuttering murderer, to deliver His people from Egypt. He raised up a woman named Deborah to rally Israel's warriors and lead them into victory. God anointed David, a teenage singing shepherd, to be a king; and an orphan, Esther, to be a queen. He designated a peasant girl, Mary, to carry the long-awaited King of kings. God commissioned Mary

Magdalene, a former demoniac, to be the Resurrection's first evangelist. He empowered Peter, a cussing fisherman, to be the church's first leader. God will use anyone from anywhere who will simply say yes to Him!

Observing the miraculous affirmation of God's Spirit on my life, my father was compelled to inquire more deeply from the Word of God regarding women in positional ministry. After an exhaustive study, he called me into his office:

"I've determined the Bible does not prohibit you from preaching and leading, Rae. If you're willing to learn, I'm willing to mentor you officially in pastoral ministry."

"Yes!" I answered.

Thirty years after my initial Holy Spirit infilling, I once again stepped onto the platform of my father's church. He had just retired and watched me ascend the stairs from the front pew. In an auditorium vastly greater than the original humble structure, I moved behind the large circular pulpit, opened my Bible, and turned the pages to the text to deliver the morning sermon. This time, however, I gave the message as lead pastor.

No matter who you are or where you are from, God is calling you. He cares not if you are a man or woman, young or old, poor or rich, black or white, or brown. He is simply looking for those with enough faith to say yes to Him. That singular and personal "yes" to God will initiate a ripple that grows into a tidal wave of His purpose. *It all starts with you saying "yes."*

For too long, we have personally and corporately waited for someone else to get the "multiculturalism" going. We've looked to the megachurch pastors, renowned evangelists, state bishops, supervisors, general overseers, and denomination presidents to initiate the process. Inclusion and oneness, however, is first a personal job. God is simply waiting for your "yes." *The* "we" will always begin with "me."

IT'S ME, IT'S ME, IT'S ME, OH LORD

The principle is this: before it can happen *through* me it must happen *in* me. More specifically, before multiculturalism can happen in my ministry, God must do His work in me individually. This is not only an essential leadership strategy but also a deeply personal spiritual activity. Paul brought this poignant truth forward as he recounted his conversion testimony and missionary directive to King Agrippa in Acts 26:

> "I have appeared to you for this purpose, to make you a minister and a witness [Jesus said]. . . . I will deliver you from the Jewish people, as well as from the Gentiles, to whom I now send you, to open their eyes, in order to turn them from darkness to light, and from the power of Satan to God, that they may receive forgiveness of sins and an inheritance among those who are sanctified by faith in Me" (vv. 16-18 NKJV).

Prior to his conversion, Paul (known then as Saul) was a religious zealot, authorized by the leading priests to persecute Jesus' followers (Acts 9:1-19). At salvation, Christ delivered Saul from his religious elitism, legalism, and prejudice against Gentiles. The Jewish leaders then hated him so greatly, they threatened his life. The animosity and rabid rejection of Paul by his Jewish brothers would have been emotionally crushing and isolating. To move into his ordained purpose, Paul had to be personally healed from the pain his Jewish brothers' hatred as well as from his bigotry against the Gentiles. Without deliverance from both, Paul could not fulfill his calling as the bridge of the Gospel from the Jews to the Gentiles. Deliverance had to begin with Paul before it could be extended to others. *Paul had to become a delivered deliverer.* And, so did I.

MAKE THE CULTURE SHIFT

The table was set in my best china, silver, crystal, and table linens. Name place-cards for each guest were positioned on the beautiful table, along with candles and a fabulous floral centerpiece. My guests would be arriving soon, so I enlisted my son and daughter to help with the final tasks of lighting the candles and plating the dinner salads. I was newly married to a brilliant Latino pastor. Together, we had big dreams for our blended, multiracial family, as well as for a blended, multicultural church. This evening, his parents, uncle, aunt, and cousin were arriving for dinner for the first time since our wedding. I wanted everything to be perfect, and it was—so far.

"Hey, honey! Get down here! Your family will be here in two minutes!" I shouted up the stairs to my husband.

"Two minutes?" he questioned, peering down from the upstairs banister at me, buttoning up his shirt.

"Hello? We said 6:30 pm! It's 6:28 now," I stated, tapping my wristwatch. "Get down here, pleeeeease!" I begged.
"Um . . . they might be a little late," he warned.

"That's okay. Five or ten minutes won't make a difference. But get down here. I need your help," I commanded.

Five minutes passed, then ten, and then fifteen, but there was no knock on the door. I began to worry, checking the food and turning down the warmer.

"Where are they? Why don't you call them and see if something has happened?" I instructed my husband.

He suddenly became fidgety and stepped out of the room. I could hear him talking to his parents in Spanish, but the sentences were spoken too rapidly for me to comprehend. He returned sheepishly with the phone in hand.

"They're just around the corner," he assured.

I narrowed my eyes and put my hands on my hips.

"What corner?"

More than thirty minutes later, his family finally arrived. I ran eagerly to the door to greet my five special guests, tearing off the apron as I went. Swinging open the door, I was greeted not by only my five family members, but also by ten other individuals who were no relation at all.

"Mija!" my mother-in-law greeted enthusiastically. "We are so excited for dinner with you!"

I kissed her and my father-in-law, then watched the procession of unknown guests follow them through my door. Turning my head slowly and dramatically toward my husband as they all marched through, he shrugged his shoulders happily and took their coats.

"Please, make yourself comfortable in the family room," I instructed my guests, and then whispered to my husband, "We need to talk."

These four simple words uttered by a wife can make even the burliest of men shudder. It matters not if he is a construction worker, plumber, professor, multimillionaire mogul, or minister. These four words will make sweat beads erupt across a man's forehead and adrenaline surge through his body.

My husband met me in the hall and immediately tried to temper the forthcoming conversation with humor.

'We' Starts With 'Me'

"Listen, Lucy—" he started.

"Not funny, Ricardo! Who are all these people? We are supposed to have five—count them, five guests—not a whole congregation!" I exclaimed, waving five fingers in the air.

"Okay. Le' me esplen it to ju," he said, purposefully emphasizing his accent to sound over-the-top ridiculous.

"We are Latinos! Whoever happens to be at the house when it's time to go to dinner, comes with us. It would have been rude in our culture to tell them to go home or leave them there at the house. So, my parents invited them to join us. Just put some water in the soup."

"We're having stuffed Cornish game hens!" I fumed.

"Then, we'll make tacos out of them!" he grinned.

So commenced my baptism into Latino culture. The irony is, I had prided myself, because of being raised as a missionary kid in Mexico, as fully prepared for living daily within the Hispanic culture. There is a big difference, however, between elegantly and periodically dipping a pedicured toe into the pool of cultural diversity and being thrown into the deep end. For the first months of my marriage and pastorate, I occasionally resembled a desperate drowning poodle. I can laugh about it now, but I discovered my image of myself as a multicultural matriarch was incongruent with reality. In too many ways, I was selfish, with a sense of cultural entitlement and superiority. God wanted me to be a change agent, but He first had to radically change me.

CULTURE SHOCK

The vision for a racially and culturally diverse church is glorious. Yet the process to fulfillment of that dream will personally and corporately challenge our traditions, preferences, values, and comfort zones. We will be tested by a different set of cultural values which, in turn, forces consideration of our true priorities. The surprise guests at dinner began the process of personal evaluation. I had to determine whether my perfectly planned table and menu were more important than laughter, bonding, and fellowship. I ended up deciding that honoring the cultural priorities of my husband and in-laws was more important than my fancy table. So, stuffed-Cornish-game-hen tacos are what we ate that night—buffet style.

When opening the ministry table to other ethnicities and cultures, our churches will be stretched. Not all will be willing to make their own cultural traditions and preferences subservient to the vision of diversity in the church. Broadening music styles, including people of color into the leadership, and adjusting budgets and facility usage will test the mettle of our iron wills. That is why God will test *you and your resolve* first. You must be able to stand up under the pressure and heat when the inevitable conflicts of values and traditions collide.

For our church, it began when we elevated our Hispanic ministries from a "department" in our Anglo church into a fully integrated partnership. Though the services remained separate because of language preference, we made room in the office, staff meetings, and on the church council, fusing the two ministries under one vision. This move was carefully preceded by vision-casting, Biblical teaching on diversity, and many meetings regarding corporate values, leadership expectations, financial boundaries, and shared facility usage.

Though the Anglo leadership was "all in" in concept, the reality of integration was a shock to some. Instead of being relegated to a corner of the campus, Latinos (and their rambunctious children) were now everywhere. Especially when they discovered the power of facility requests submitted six months in advance! Suddenly the Anglo church did not have an automatic preference for dates. We had to learn partnership, and *true partnership means equal opportunity, access, and authority.* This was more than what some of my White congregants could handle, especially when it meant they no longer had the facility and budgetary superiority.

"But we've always had our ladies' events on that weekend!" Sister Shirley complained with indignation.

"Yes, I understand. And, that is why we contacted you over a month ago and encouraged you to get your facility request in for it. The Latino women's ministry requested that date as well, and they put their request in months ago. We called you several times about it, remember?" I reminded.

"Those people are taking over!" she exclaimed. "It's just not right!"

"*Those* people?" I echoed back. "You mean your precious sisters in the Lord who cooked you chicken soup and cleaned your house when you were sick a few months back? Is that who you're talking about, Sister Shirley?" She lowered her eyes and fumbled with her tissue.

"It's hard, Pastor. Everything is changing."

"Yes, it is hard. But we promised God we would give up some things so we could open our hearts to the nations. This is the hard part, but it's worth it." I paused and then forwarded an idea.

"What would you think of doing a great big, combined women's event?" I suggested. "Let's think differently! It's not us and them anymore. It's 'we' now. You're so brilliant, Shirley. I think you can rally all the women and make this the best and biggest event we've ever had! I'll help, and . . . I'll double the budget." She was in.

The culture shock was amplified when, over the course of about eighteen months, we hired three African-Americans to take the lead in church administration, accounting, and worship and the arts. We expected some adjustment and discomfort as people got accustomed to new leadership and an infusion of Black culture into our services and structures. What I didn't expect, however, was the hidden hatred their empowerment exposed, even in some of our top leadership—Latino and Anglo. Two of these new staff members had already been serving in the church and left big paychecks to join our team. The other had been a guest artist in our services numerous times. Apparently, it was one thing to worship and serve alongside African-Americans, but another thing completely to work under their authority. That's when real "ugly" came out. I was even told by one elderly Latino couple I was being entranced by black witches and warlocks. *Prejudice is an equal opportunity employer.*

Our new staff members were educated, capable, gifted, and gracious individuals whose character rose above the nonsense, and whose nobility refused to take offense. So, we kept moving forward with the vision. Those who wouldn't rise up dropped out. Yet, it tested my own fortitude in maintaining the Lord's uncompromised multicultural vision.

God wants to use us to be His change agents in the world. Dr. Dave Martin says, "Change starts inside you, not around you." Deliverance begins with us, not "them." Like Paul, we must allow God to bring personal deliverance to our souls. Where there has been elitism, let there be inclusion. Where there has been wounding, let there be restoration. Where there has been bitterness, let there be reconciliation. We must be delivered to deliver and be healed, so we can heal others. We must change to bring change and be different, so we can make a difference.

AUDACIOUS ANANIAS

While on the road to Damascus, Saul was blinded; and then led to an amazing man of simple obedience and grace, Ananias, who willingly became the conduit of God's healing (Acts 9:1-19). Ananias only gets a few verses in this chapter. The Lord didn't blind him with a bright light or change his name. There is no record of Ananias being sent to far-away places, nor do we hear that he suffered arrest, floggings, stoning, imprisonment, or shipwreck. Rather than giving Ananias an assignment to change the entire world, the Lord gave him an assignment to change the world for just *one person:* Saul. Yet, by changing the life of one person, Ananias ended up impacting the entire world. Consider this: Without an Ananias, who dared to say yes to God, we would not have Paul, who dared to preach and write to us. Paul became daring for Jesus because Ananias was daring for Jesus over *just one soul*! His singular impact was so far-reaching, every non-Jewish Christian owes him an immense debt of gratitude. Because of Ananias, Saul became Paul, the apostle to the Gentiles and writer of much of the New Testament. Ananias illuminates the impact of one person who dares to say yes to God.

ONE FOR ALL, AND ALL FOR ONE

The story is told of a grandfather and his grandson walking on the beach together. Starfish had washed up that morning by the thousands and lay helpless in the scorching sun. As they walked, the grandfather picked up one and carefully tossed it back into the water. A few steps farther, he picked up another starfish and did the same. The young boy viewed the overwhelming number of starfish on the beach and asked, "Grandpa, you can't save them all. Why even try?"

The grandfather grabbed another starfish and put it in his grandson's hand.

"Throw it in," he instructed. So, the boy obeyed.

"See, it does matter. It matters to that one."

Multicultural ministry rarely begins with a crowd. It begins with the "one." Your church will most likely not suddenly fill up one Sunday with people of diverse backgrounds and ethnicities. A culturally inclusive ministry begins first on the personal level, with the renewing of our minds and the expansion of our hearts. God will purge our souls of bigotry, bitterness, and superiority, and replace them with His grace, forgiveness, and humility. He will widen our capacity to love and serve others. Then, and only then, God will connect us to the one significant "gateway" person who will open the door to an entire community.

ONE PLUS ONE EQUALS 1,000

Driving toward the church campus one morning, I noticed four dark Black women dressed in colorful elaborate dresses and heads wrapped in matching fabric, walking on the sidewalk together. With several active children in tow, and infants cuddled up in slings on their backs, they made their way to a large apartment building and then disappeared from my view. I noticed more people of African descent in traditional clothing as the weeks went by. After asking city officials about them, I discovered the government was settling African refugees from several countries in apartments within a five-mile radius of the church. I had always wanted to go to Africa, but instead, God had brought Africa to me!

"Oh, Lord! Show me how to connect with these people!" I pleaded in prayer.

A few weeks later, I spied a woman in traditional African clothing sitting at the back of the auditorium during one of our Sunday services. After preaching, I headed straight for her and introduced myself. Mother Rose was a Liberian refugee. She lived in Phoenix and attended a church there. The Lord had spoken to her that morning to drive down to Tucson and attend our Sunday service. This mighty woman of God was the birthing mother of several African refugee churches. She would visit the refugee apartment blocks, hold Bible studies, and lead people to Christ. Once she had a houseful of people, she would look for a church and pastor who would embrace them. I was, and still am, astounded by the wondrous faith and servanthood of this amazing woman of God.

"They can come here!" I exclaimed. "We will start an African Fellowship."

But first, it was necessary to build trust and relationships with the refugee community. So, we enlisted the help of a couple of gifted women and an organization experienced in refugee connections. We began to meet African refugees at the airport, assist with basic supplies for their apartments, show them how to get around the city, and teach them English. By serving the need, it opened the door to relationships. Within a few months, we started a church! We were all so excited for the day we would formally launch the African Fellowship. Nigerian women in the group had purchased a traditional Nigerian dress and bright orange headdress for me to wear that day. I wore them proudly to all our services that Sunday, though I noticed quite a few giggles by the Africans at the sight of me. After, praying for the new pastor and his spouse, and preaching an inaugurating sermon, we enjoyed a homemade African buffet, with the delicacies and recipes of eight different African nations. Mother Rose sat proudly beside me the entire time, content with all God had done.

After almost everyone had left, she and several women tentatively approached me.

"Pastor Rae, we must tell you something very important," they said cautiously, with serious expressions. I tensed, wondering what terrible thing would tarnish this wonderful day. They hesitated, looking pensively at each other.

"Don't worry, just tell me," I entreated, bracing myself.

"You have worn your Nigerian hat backwards all day! It's supposed to go the other way around!"

I threw my head back and roared with laughter, thinking of all the pictures that had been taken and sent around the world of me in backward Nigerian headdress. They all laughed with me until tears streamed down our cheeks and our stomachs ached. A backwards hat I could handle!

As members of the African Fellowship traveled back to their families in the refugee camps in Africa, they began to win people to the Lord there. On one of his trips back home, our African pastor, Safari Kalunga, sent me photos of churches filled with precious people,

"Mother, you and Mother Rose now have African children in Uganda, Liberia, and the Congo too!" was his caption.

'We' Starts With 'Me'

One woman became our gateway to the African continent.

Jesus modeled this effective strategy throughout the Gospels when reaching a new people group. For instance, in John 4, He began His Samaritan ministry by connecting with a lonely woman at a well. She became the gateway who opened the entire Samaritan city of Sychar to Christ. In the region of the Gadarenes, as recorded in Mark 5:1-20, Jesus ministered deliverance to the resident graveyard demoniac, and in the process, stampeded a herd of pigs right off a cliff. The people were not yet ready for this miracle-working and demon-dispatching Messiah. Jesus graciously left the area, but not without first sending the former demoniac back home to testify about what God had done for him. The man preached about Jesus throughout the ten cities of the Decapolis. So, when Christ returned to the area in Mark 6:53, He was eagerly received by the crowd, because the former demoniac had opened wide the gates to the region through his powerful testimony. God will deal with the one (you) to reach one, so that one can reach all! *All for one, and one for all.*

We see these principles played out through the extraordinary ministry of Ananias in Acts 9:10-14:

> In Damascus there was a disciple named Ananias. The Lord called to him in a vision, "Ananias!" "Yes, Lord," he answered. The Lord told him, "Go to the house of Judas on Straight Street and ask for man from Tarsus named Saul, for he is praying. In a vision he has seen a man named Ananias come and place his hands on him to restore his sight." "Lord," Ananias answered, "I have heard many reports about this man and all the harm he has done to your holy people in Jerusalem. And he has come here with authority from the chief priests to arrest all who call on you name."

TO REACH THE ONE, KNOW GOD

The most attractive quality about you to other people groups will not be your astounding knowledge of God but, instead, your intimate relationship with Him. On the road to Damascus, Saul heard the voice of Jesus. Shortly after, Ananias heard from Jesus too; but unlike Saul, Ananias had a full conversation with the Lord. Ananias had such an intimate relationship with Christ, he dared to argue with God. We all know there is no winning an argument with God (truly, who would want to!). However, Ananias was in such a close relationship with the Lord, he recognized His voice and dialogued with Him. Some think the ability to hear and talk with God makes a person crazy. To me, it is even crazier *not* to hear and talk with God!

Abraham negotiated with God over Lot; Moses interceded over Israel's sin; and David whined, complained, questioned, prayed, and praised. The ability to dialogue with God is a sign of intimate relationship and proximity. Notice the difference between Saul the Pharisee and Ananias, the servant: Saul had a religious belief system about God, but Ananias had a living relationship. Saul knew all about God as a Pharisee, but Ananias actually knew God.

When Jesus conversed with the Samaritan woman in John 4:22, He told her, "You Samaritans worship what you do not know."

The Samaritans had stories about God and traditions of liturgical worship, but they didn't know Him. People around the world have been saturated with and stunted by religious rules and regulations, but they are hungry for what is authentic and transforming. They are longing for a relationship with God. An intimate relationship *with* God is a prerequisite to having an impact *for* God. Moses cried out in Exodus 33:13, "Show me Your way, that I may know You" (NKJV). David prayed in Psalm 42:1-2, "As the deer pants for the water brooks, so my soul pants for You, O God. My soul thirsts for God, for the living God. When shall I come and appear before God?" (NKJV). Paul later echoed this in his writing, reflecting the intimacy he must have seen in Ananias:

> I consider everything a loss because of the surpassing worth of knowing Christ Jesus my Lord, for whose sake I have lost all things. I consider them garbage, that I may gain Christ… I want to know Christ—yes, to know the power of his resurrection and participation in his sufferings (Philippians 3:8-10).

To know Christ became the primary passion of Paul's heart. He exhorted believers in Ephesians 1:17, "I keep asking that the God of our Lord Jesus Christ, the glorious Father, may give you the Spirit of wisdom and revelation, so that you may know him better."

It is easy as ministers to allow the rhythm of ministry to blunt our senses to our daily need for fresh faith, fresh oil, fresh fire, a fresh word. When was the last time you wept or leapt in His presence, without a long agenda, but simply in awe and wonder? God wants to rekindle our relationship with Him until our passion for Him burns like a fire. John Wesley is credited as saying, "I get alone with God in prayer. He sets me on fire. The people come out to watch me burn." As a bonfire attracts a crowd, so a fiery passion for Jesus is captivating. Yet, a fire that has gone out smolders and stinks, and discharges a noxious, irritating smoke. It is repelling, not compelling. A rekindled intimate relationship with God will attract that one person who will transform the entire context of our ministries.

TO REACH THE ONE, OBEY GOD

Ananias was commanded to go, and go he did! Imagine how scary it must have been for him to obey God's minutely detailed instructions. He was being asked by God to declare Christ to a man who was persecuting Christians. Yet, Ananias displayed unparalleled surrender and resolute obedience that manifested in his audacious boldness. Ananias was able, because of obedience, to walk authoritatively into that house on Straight Street, lay his hands on this murderer and declare, "Brother Saul, the Lord Jesus, who appeared to you on the road as you were coming here—has sent me so that you may see again and be filled with the Holy Spirit" (Acts 9:17).

God backed Ananias up with the gift of healing, deliverance, and restoration, and Saul was miraculously transformed to Paul. When we determine to obey God, even in the risky and bewildering, He will set our feet in places, and with people, we never dreamed possible, and He back us up with all His provision and miraculous might.

> Now to Him who is able to do immeasurably more than all we ask or imagine, according to His power that is at work within us, to Him be glory in the church and in Christ Jesus throughout all generations (Ephesians 3:20-21).

TO REACH THE ONE, FORGIVE

When reading Acts 9, we hear fear and trepidation in Ananias' voice. It is likely Ananias knew some of the people Saul had tortured. What God was asking him to do would not only risk his life but possibly the lives of his own family and friends. This had to be very difficult, but what was conceivably even more difficult was Ananias being sent by God to minister reconciliation and forgiveness to Saul. Do you realize God wants to use you to minister His lavish grace and boundless forgiveness to the very people who have caused you the greatest threat, disrespect, and pain? This is the ministry of reconciliation:

> Therefore, if anyone is in Christ, the new creation has come: The old has gone, the new is here! All this is from God, who reconciled us to himself through Christ and gave us the ministry of reconciliation: that God was reconciling the world to himself in Christ, not counting men's sins against them. And He has committed to us the message of reconciliation. We are therefore Christ's ambassadors (2 Corinthians 5:17-20).

To be Christ's ambassador of reconciliation, we must first be willing to forgive, "not counting men's sins against them." For God cannot send us to extend His freeing grace if we're still fastened to hurt, bitterness, fear, and unforgiveness. We cannot minister His boundless love while still bound up by hate.

Astonishingly, Jesus had already forgiven Saul for his atrocious sins. Christ had died in advance for Saul, paying the penalty for a man who would hunt down His precious people and kill them. That is God's incredible, incomprehensible, and uncomfortable grace! Grace so abundant and free, lavish and forgiving, it had to boggle the mind of this devoted follower of Jesus. Yet, Ananias chose to replicate and imitate what Jesus had done. I wonder if Paul was thinking about Ananias when he wrote,

> Therefore, be imitators of God as dear children. And walk in love, as Christ also has loved us and given Himself for us, an offering and sacrifice to God for a sweet-smelling aroma (Ephesians 5:1-2 NKJV).

Mother Teresa said, "If we really want to love we must learn how to forgive." Forgiveness does not excuse others' actions. Instead, forgiveness stops their actions from destroying our heart and purpose. Ananias chose to forgive Saul for his hate, bigotry, and violence not because Saul deserved it, but because Ananias was daring enough to act like Jesus. Doing so positioned Ananias to be promoted from some obscure, fearful, reactionary, bitter man into the disciple who became Christ's ambassador of grace and forgiveness.

Indira Gandhi stated, "Forgiveness is a virtue of the brave." Ananias became the one who opened the door to the Gentile world because Ananias was brave enough to forgive and minister reconciliation to Saul. We see God's intention for restoration revealed even in the meticulous details of God's directions to Ananias: "Go to the house of Judas on Straight Street and ask for a man from Tarsus named Saul" (Acts 9:10-11).

The name *Ananias* means, "God is gracious." *House of Judas* means literally, "house of praise." *Straight Street* is a place of "realignment of direction," where "the crooked road is made straight" (see Isaiah 40:3; Luke 3:4b). God's grace was poured out on Saul to realign the course of His life and dramatically change his identity. Paul would then live for the glory and praise of God. God used a simple man named Ananias, who knew the Lord and would obey Him, to forgive as Jesus did. Ananias' amazing ability to forgive and minister is so comprehensive, he called Saul, "Brother Saul" (Acts 9:17). Only by daring to forgive does a murderer, tormentor, abuser, and bigot become a brother.

My friends, God is about to pour out grace and forgiveness on some of your most vicious enemies, and He wants to use you as His conduit. Perhaps a resentment was instilled after you or your family experienced hurt by White people, or someone of African, Arabic, Asian, or Latino descent. The devastation of a man's abuse or the humiliation of a church lady's gossip may have made you apprehensive, reactionary, or bitter. Despite this, God is calling you to be an agent of change. *But you can't be a change agent with a chip on your shoulder!* Becoming a change agent starts by choosing to forgive in the face of bias, inequity, prejudice, and racism. It takes more strength to forgive than it does to acquiesce to hate and bitterness. Forgiveness and love are risky. They demand great personal courage and a solid trust in God. Dr. Martin Luther King Jr. said, "Forgiveness is not an occasional act, it is a constant attitude." He said this while encountering vicious racism and violence that eventually cost him his life. His message still challenges us today to become change agents by bravely and intentionally cultivating a heart of forgiveness. *To reach the one, forgive.*

There is no way Ananias could have known the impact this religious zealot, Saul, would end up having throughout history. The late Archbishop Desmond Tutu said, "God places us in the world as His fellow workers—agents of transfiguration." We will impact the nations if we will (1) recognize, "*We* begins with *Me*," and (2) understand before multicultural ministry can happen *through* us, it must first happen *in* us.

9

Forward Vision

My feet were frozen in my ski boots as I shivered in the snow—not from the cold, but because I was paralyzed in fear. After two days of absurdly expensive lessons, I was still better equipped for sipping hot cocoa by the fire than sliding down icy slopes. Now petrified in terror, halfway down a black-diamond ski run, I plotted cold revenge on all the people who had told me it would be easy. Diabolically deceptive, the beginning of the run had been wide and flat, and I'd glided back and forth euphoric in my newfound athletic abilities. Yet, the slope had lured me into false confidence and then suddenly plunged into an icy descent.

"Shift your weight onto your downhill ski. Eyes forward and lean into it!" my friend yelled from several yards down the slope, as advanced skiers whizzed past me on both sides.

"I can't!" I moaned.

"Yes, you can!" she demanded.

"No! I can't!" I shouted back angrily. "It goes against everything in me to lean toward a downhill drop. It's insanity: completely contradictory to natural wisdom!"

"If you don't, you'll stay stuck here. You won't be able to move forward!" she reasoned.

I still wasn't budging. So, she took off her goggles with a sigh and shook the frost from them.

"What's your plan, Pastor? Are we staying the night here?" she teased, blinking from the soft flakes of snow landing on her eyelashes.

"Yes, we are! Get a tent, firewood, and some s'mores," I fumed.

With that, she chopped her skis into the snow horizontally and laboriously planked her way up the hill to me.

"Okay, we'll do it together. If you fall, you'll fall on me and we'll roll down the hill as one big snowball." We giggled together at the thought.

"Look—there's an easy path across and back that leads us all the way down the hill. Do you see it, now?"

I nodded affirmatively.

"Great! Now—eyes forward, lean in!" she coaxed.

I finally overcame my fear, and slowly traversed the treacherous drop. With the patient assistance of my friend, I made it all the way down that black-diamond slope. Yet, movement only came after I had determined it was scarier to stay there all night, perched perilously on a frozen mogul fighting off wolves, than it was to fall headlong down the hill.

EYES FORWARD, LEAN IN

It is more precarious for the church to stay immobilized in a segregated and sickly state than to traverse the undefined terrain of partnership together. Our divine mission to communicate the Gospel to all nations is too critical and urgent for hesitation. Multicultural cohesion beckons us forward . . . but where do we start?

Forward Vision

The Apostle Paul gives us understanding and direction in 2 Corinthians 5, speaking first to our need for renewed vision and fresh perspective:

> So from now on we regard no one from a worldly point of view. Though we once regarded Christ in this way, we do so no longer. Therefore, if anyone is in Christ, the new creation has come: The old has gone, the new is here! (vv. 16-17).

Multicultural ministry requires a new perspective. Speaking to the culturally diverse community of believers in Corinth, Paul's primary message was to shift their perspective from earthly to heavenly. In verse 16, he emphasized our worldly view is fatally flawed. Our worldly traditions, biases, and wounds have marred and muddied our ability to see people the way God sees them. A tainted or skewed view of others will cause us to disfigure them or mistake them for something or someone they are not.

20/20 VISION

It is unpleasant for me to confess I'm getting older. Part of this reality is my eyes are not as keen as they once were. For years, my children prompted me to go to the optometrist for glasses. I resisted, reluctant to surrender my last remnant of youthfulness to the inevitable granny bifocals. One day, after speaking at a conference, I spied dear friends across the auditorium. Eager to reconnect, I yelled out their names and waved, but strangely they didn't respond. Somewhat irked by their lack of enthusiasm in seeing me, I moved through the crowd toward them.

"Keith and Juanita, it has been such a long time since I've seen you!" I exclaimed, slowly making my way to them.

They, however, did not reciprocate my excitement but instead looked at each other perplexed. Finally reaching them, I joyfully embraced both in a confident, wholehearted hug. They were awkwardly stiff, so I pulled away, confused and a little irritated. Only when I was two feet from their faces did I realize these individuals were not Keith and Juanita!

I made the appointment for glasses.

We also need new lenses that will give us a fresh view of our harvest field. Paul said, "The old has gone, the new is here!" So, our old way of looking at things needs to change. It's time for a divine lens upgrade. After my eye exam, the optometrist told me I needed not bifocals, but trifocals! I was horrified, conjuring up images of the old church mothers: grey hair up in a tight bun and round spectacles on the tip of their nose. I was delighted when the eye doc told me I could get fashion-forward frames for my, ugh . . . trifocals.

"What in the world are trifocals anyway?" I questioned.

"They are eyeglasses with specially cut lenses that correct your view from three different regions," he answered.

I believe we need "trifocals" for multicultural ministry too. We need (1) a new view of the harvest, (2) divine revelation, and (3) cultural clarity. Let's try out these lenses together:

1. **We need a new view of the harvest.** The worldly view we've grown up with has distorted and misrepresented the individuals and people groups whom we are called to impact. *If we don't view people properly, we can't serve them effectively.* For some of us, acquiring a fresh heavenly perspective may mean we address generations-long biases based on culture and traditions. For others, a new view may necessitate the hard work of

forgiving those who were responsible for the pain and injustice of prejudice. Yet, the benefits of renewed vision will allow us to truly "open [our] eyes and look at the fields! They are ripe for harvest" (John 4:35). Heavenly 20/20 vision will give us the ability to see people and our last-days harvest-field as Jesus does.

2. *We need divine revelation.* I'm a firm believer in our need for supernatural revelation and direction from God, especially when it comes to leading His church. God has divine strategies for initiating cross-cultural relationships and integrating people groups into our ministries. This truth is evidenced repeatedly in the Book of Acts. Philip the evangelist was supernaturally transported by the Holy Spirit so he could connect with an Ethiopian eunuch in Acts 8:26-39. Peter was given a vivid vision in Acts 10 prompting his outreach to a Roman centurion, Cornelius, and ultimately to the Gentiles. Paul and his crew were consistently guided in their missionary ventures by visions and dreams, as well as the direct voice of the Holy Spirit. The Apostles were reliably led by the Holy Spirit in how they were to reach diverse cultures, lands, and peoples in a supernatural fashion. They had a daily expectation of God's miraculous guidance. So why wouldn't we expect the same, and even greater, in these latter days? "Jesus Christ is the same yesterday, today and forever" (Hebrews 13:8 NKJV).

We often walk around with eyes wide open to earthly realities, while our eyes are shut tight to God's supernatural certainties. In 2 Kings 6, when Elisha's servant panicked at the sight of Aram's army encamped around him, Elisha discerned the problem was with the servant's earthly perspective. Elisha prayed simply, "Open his eyes, Lord, so that he may see. Then the Lord opened the servant's eyes, and he looked and saw the hills full of horses and chariots of fire all around Elisha" (v. 17).

HE HAD TO GO THERE

While frozen on that harrowing ski slope, I was blinded and paralyzed by fear. All I could see was the treacherous descent, my lack of athletic ability, and my inevitable death-plunge to the bottom. Intimidation is utterly blinding, isn't it? Though we may possess a deep desire to see diversity on church platforms and in pews, knowing where and how to start is often overwhelming. So, in frustration, we may choose to remain in ethnic singularity, frozen by the possibility of failure. On the frosty incline, however, my fearless friend had a clearer and broader view of our icy landscape than I did. She saw the path across the slope that could be safely traversed back and forth. It was there all the time. I just needed her help to see it.

In the same way, clear pathways, divine opportunities, and heavenly strategies await you, if you will simply ask the Holy Spirit to open your eyes and embolden your heart. For the Lord knows your ministry landscape even better than you do! He understands the intricacies and challenges of where and whom you serve, as surely as He understands the complicated cultures within the region. He knows the pathway forward to your greatest ministry impact and influence. So, ask the Lord to open your eyes and He will surely do it!

3. *We need cultural clarity.* After we acquire a new view of our harvest and ask the Holy Spirit for divine revelation, it is imperative we develop cultural clarity.

"What's wrong with this stupid phone!" I exclaimed, exasperated.

Some would say I'm technologically challenged, which is just a nice way of saying my smartphone is significantly smarter than I am. I can hardly program my own coffee pot for a morning brew, let alone negotiate the technology of my iPhone, Alexa, or the TV.

"What's it doing now, Mom?" asked the resident computer tech, my teenage daughter, Gigi.

"It's doing this flashy thing and glitching," I grumbled.

"When's the last time you updated and reset it?" she asked.

"Umm . . . what's that?" I blinked cluelessly.

"Mom, are you serious? No wonder it's being weird! Apple literally sends you a software update in your settings. You've gotta initiate the update and accept the terms and conditions. Then you'll get the new features, and the phone will stop glitching. You're supposed to update and reset your phone every once in a while, to keep it working properly. I can't believe you haven't done that!"

She laughed, incredulous at my ignorance, and immediately grabbed the phone away to start the updates.

People of my generation have settled comfortably into our original ministry methods and styles of preaching, counseling, administrating, evangelizing, and leadership. Our initial ministry "programming" has worked effectively for years within the culture we have served. Lately, however, it may have started "glitching" like my iPhone, becoming less compatible with this newer, ethnically diverse and technologically advanced generation. To *glitch* means to "experience an irregularity or setback due to a malfunction or system irrelevance." If you're still breathing, God intends for you to function ministerially at full capacity and clarity. You were not destined for irrelevance unless you sentence yourself to it.

Culture is an ever-transforming living organism of thought and expression. Every culture, regardless of its ethnic or national origin, adapts to the impact of crisis, poverty, and hardship as well as to technology and opportunity. For instance, my grandparents grew up as hard-working blue-collar family people. Their generation developed new values, skills, language, traditions, and anxieties after experiencing the Great Depression and World War 2. Because of the trauma, their generational culture was dramatically different from those prior. My parents' culture, on the other hand, was shaped by the prosperity boom following WW2, the civil rights movement, political assassinations, the Vietnam War, and the moon landing. It was necessary for my father to repackage the message of God's grace so people like the hippies could grasp its power.

Updating your methodology of ministry is not a compromise of godly living or a dilution of the steadfast, infallible, and unchanging Word of God. It is, instead, learning a new language for effectively communicating the Gospel and discipling the nations. As a case in point, I've heard well-meaning, yet historically ill-informed preachers declare, "We preach the real and true Word of God at my church: the King James Version of the Bible!" The King James Version was written over 400 years ago in medieval English. So, if the young man taking your order at Chick-fil-A does not do so in old English "thee's and thou's," it means the current language has changed. The power of God's Word should not be obscured by antiquated colloquialisms and linguistics. Instead, should be presented in present-day language so it's fully comprehended by present-day culture.

One of the primary purposes of Pentecost was that "each one heard their own language being spoken" (Acts 2:6). Language is more than only words. Language is expressed in culture through customs, art, music, dress, and technology. To have greater cultural clarity, it is essential to regularly download new information, ministry applications, updated language, and methods that will function well in this high-tech, racially diverse generation. Doing so will help to widen and clarify the circle of our ministry influence and impact. Technically speaking, we need to "refresh our ministry software" by intentionally seeking to educate ourselves and expand cross-cultural relationships. Reading, research, taking classes, going to conferences, and cultural exposure brings expanded vision. At the back of this book, I've listed several resources you can access to get you started.

The greatest source of eye-opening cultural clarity comes from cultural immersion, like extended mission trips, and by developing cross-cultural relationships here at home. Sitting across a table and talking with a person of different skin tones and backgrounds, is marvelously illuminating. Tony Evans said, "Authentic oneness comes as an outgrowth of shared lives, not simply through, a cross-cultural experience here or there."[1] Face to face and eye to eye, there is a transfer of thought, ideas, heart, and passion that cannot be found in any book or lecture. "Relationships are the true currency of the Kingdom," says Bishop Mitchell Corder. How true! Relationships are a mutual transference of life that awakens the spirit and animates faith; they widen vision, brighten purpose, and motivate motion.

1,000 CUPS OF TEA

My office phone rang, jolting me from study. I'd been working on a sermon series and was deep in thought, endeavoring to write a few message outlines for our season's ministry theme. I had asked not to be disturbed, so Drew, our young intern, who was manning the reception desk, spoke apologetically:

"Pastor Rae, I know you asked not to be disturbed, but there is a man here who says he needs to see you."

HE HAD TO GO THERE

There were no scheduled appointments on my calendar that afternoon so I could study. Drew was surprisingly adept for his young age at referring individuals in crisis or walk-ins to staff pastors when I was unavailable. The tension I heard in his voice gave me pause.

"Drew, please excuse yourself and come chat with me a minute," I directed.

He seated our unscheduled guest in the lobby and walked down the corridor to my office.

"What's wrong? Who is it?" I asked, peering over the books stacked on my big study desk. "Can you help him make an appointment for another time? I really need this research time."

I then realized I was asking questions at a machine-gun rate without pausing to hear any answers.

"Sorry. Go ahead."

"Well, he looks and talks like an Arab sort of. His name is . . . um . . . ." He looked down to read a name scrawled onto a post-it note, then continued.

"Rafiq Mag . . . umm . . . Magdi. That's it—Magdi. He is super polite but, Pastor, he really wants to see you. He says he has been praying and was told by the Lord to come here," he shrugged. "I'm not sure what to do."

I sighed and looked back longingly to my unfinished sermon notes.

"It's okay I'll come out and see what's up. Tell him I'll be out in a minute," I instructed, trying to buy some time to stretch from being hunched over my books and to freshen my face.

A few minutes later, I entered our church office lobby to find a distinguished bearded man of Arabic descent, dressed in a traditional neatly pressed white cotton "thawb." On seeing me, he rose and extended his hand.

"My name is Rafiq Magdi. I am a professor at the U of A. I apologize for disturbing you, Pastor," he said, bowing his head in respect, then continued.

"I was praying, and the Lord directed me to you. Would you allow me to share my vision with you?" he asked.

Normally, I would have rerouted him to another staff pastor, or scheduled an appointment at a more convenient time. However, I felt the strong pressing of the Holy Spirit to give him time. A good amount of Jesus' most powerful miracles began as divine interruptions. So, I agreed to talk and led him to my office with Drew, the intern, following warily behind us. After he was seated, I quietly told Drew to offer our guest something to drink, then shut down the lobby, and sit visibly in the secretary's office connected to mine. Both doors were left ajar for propriety's sake. Drew asked the professor if he would like coffee or tea. He smiled broadly at this and again bowed his head respectfully.

"You win the trust of an Arab with one thousand cups of tea!" he exclaimed.

"Well, Professor, then we better get started!" I laughed.

That first of one thousand cups of tea began a wonderful friendship and ministry partnership in the city to Arabic people. A Christian who fled from persecution in Saudi Arabia, Professor Magdi had moved his family to the United States and settled in my hometown of Tucson. While teaching at the university, he attracted the interest of many Arabic refugee students and subsequently won them to Christ. However, not one church in the city had welcomed them into their fellowship. Though a decade had passed since the Twin Towers fell on 9/11, fear and loathing for Arabic people ran rampant in the area, even in the churches. I had witnessed this animosity personally at a city-wide pastors' luncheon just a month prior.

"Did you hear the city is allowing Muslims from Afghanistan, Iraq, and other Arabic nations to settle here?" said a round-faced pastor as he gulped down spaghetti.

"No way! Are you kidding me?" said another dressed in suit and tie across from him.

"Yeah! They're allowing all these Muslims to come here to the desert because of our climate and southwestern culture. They say they'll acclimate better here," the first pastor responded, wiping red sauce from his chin.

"My Lord! We can't allow that. I have a relationship with the mayor. We should go together and talk to him as city pastors. We need to stop them from coming here ASAP!" a pastor's wife sitting next to me exclaimed, as the others at the table agreed, nodding their heads vigorously.

"Why don't we want them here?" I asked. At this, they all turned and stared at me in shock.

As one of only two female pastors in the city, I was rarely invited to these events, even though the church I led was among the largest in the region. The ministers at the table had already exhibited an uncomfortable and strained tolerance at my presence during the luncheon. Now, I had confirmed their suspicions about lady pastors!

"Because they're going to bring their religion and violence into our city, that's why!" the first pastor bristled. I considered this for a moment, and then dared to bring up what I felt was the more germane issue.

"But what if God is bringing them here so we can introduce them to Jesus?" I suggested.

They unanimously rolled their eyes at me, as the spaghetti-eating pastor waved his hand dismissively and changed the subject. *They* may have dismissed my words that day, but *God* did not. He arranged an opportunity for me to live those words out loud. Professor Magdi was that God-opportunity.

"Pastor Rae, I have led several young Muslim students to the Lord," explained Professor Magdi.

"We have nowhere to go for worship and discipleship. They are too afraid to come into the churches after a couple of bad experiences. I would like to start a church for them near the university. But we would like it to be more than a church. I want to start an 'Arabian Oasis'—a cultural center for Arabic students and families. From there we will build our church. I have already started saving from my own means, but I need spiritual covering, relational support, and financial partnership. I have heard about your love for different peoples and cultures. Would you open your heart to us?" Professor Magdi pleaded.

"Yes, we will," I answered resolutely.

And yes, we did.

Put on the trifocals of multicultural ministry so God can, in turn, grant you a fresh view of your harvest field, His divine revelation and guidance, and an expanded cultural clarity. The Apostle Paul said it this way:

I pray the eyes of your heart may be enlightened in order that you may know the hope to which he has called you, the riches of his glorious inheritance in his holy people and his incomparably great power for us who believe (Ephesians 1:18-19a).

Endnotes

1 Tony Evans, *Oneness Embraced*

10

From Ambivalence to Ambassadors

Our mission is undeniably urgent, so we cannot afford to fail. The lives of this generation and those to come will stand or fall based upon our success or failure. There is nothing more important that can be achieved during our lifetimes than this God-given mandate. It is a mission so significant Jesus reiterated it five times, in five different ways, and in five books of the Bible.

- Matthew 28:19—"Therefore, go and make disciples of all the nations, baptizing them in the name of the Father and the Son and the Holy Spirit" (NLT).

- Mark 16:15—"Go into all the world and preach the Good News to everyone" (NLT).

- Luke 24:47—"And repentance for the forgiveness of sins will be preached in his name to all nations, beginning at Jerusalem."

- John 17:18—"Just as you sent me into the world, I am sending them into the world" (NLT).

- Acts 1:8—"But you will receive power when the Holy Spirit comes on you; and you will be my witnesses in Jerusalem, and in all Judea and Samaria, and to the ends of the earth."

Christ desires we emulate His vision and mission-minded earthly ministry. He said at the age of 12, "I must be about my Father's business" Luke 2:49 (NKJV). From that moment on, His mission fueled his footsteps forward to the cross at Golgotha, where he declared, "It is finished!" (John 19:30).

Before ascending to His Father, He passed the mission to us.

MISSION-MADE

God looked down through the corridor of time and chose you and me to live and serve Him in this very day. He knit together our form, built in our talents, blew into us His own breath, and poured His anointing on us. No one is designed or better built to reach this generation than we are. The Apostle Paul understood he had been specifically formed to function in his generation for the cause of Christ. Paul said, "My life is worth nothing to me unless I use it for finishing the work assigned me by the Lord Jesus—the work of telling others the Good News about the wonderful grace of God" (Acts 20:24 NLT).

We were intentionally made by God for this moment and this mission.

MISSION-MINDED

The English word for *mission* comes from the Latin word for *sending*. Jesus said, "As the Father has sent me, I am sending you" (John 20:21).

We are being sent to the *whole* world—not to one ethnicity only but to the nations. When Christ commands to go to the nations, He is talking about every tribe and tongue—not simply going across a government-drawn border. He is calling us to our Black neighbors, our Arabic neighbors, and our Latino and

Asian neighbors within the community and region in which He has placed us.

Jesus intentionally marched his disciples into Samaritan territory in John 4 so they would comprehend their mission was bigger than their own backyard, or their singular culture. The Holy Spirit enforced an enlargement of Peter's ministry focus from only to the Jews to include Gentiles in Acts 10. Paul regarded himself as the Apostle to the Gentiles, yet he consistently sought out Jews living in the regions he visited and shared the Gospel with them as well. Leaders in the early church were positioned in cities as pastors, elders, and deacons with the expectation they would serve the diverse demographic of that community. The missional principle is simply this: Latinos are not called to lead only other Latinos. People of African and Asian descent are commissioned by the Holy Spirit to minister to other races and cultures. Anglos are also called to embrace and serve diverse people groups in the area where God has planted us, and not just those across the ocean. This is the wonder of our Great Commission: We are called not only to our own specific race, but to everyone within the sphere of our city and community, as well as to other nations.

'HERE AM I, SEND ME NEXT DOOR'

Recent global migration has so changed American and international ethnic demographics that the whole world is now living within our local communities or, more specifically, next door. This makes multicultural ministry not only Christ's missional mandate, but a practical necessity if we are to impact our own neighborhood, let alone our nation. We are presently in one of the most spectacular global migrations ever recorded in history, making for individual nations that are more ethnically and culturally diverse than any period in modern times. A study published by the United Nations Department of Economic and Social Affairs, reports there were around 281 million international migrants in the world in 2020. Europe hosted approximately 87 million international immigrants, and Asia around 86 million. These regions were followed by North America, Africa, Latin America, and the Caribbean.

According to the Center for Immigration Studies, in November 2021 the U.S. immigration population had grown to 46.2 million. This is the highest number of immigrants ever recorded in any government survey or census in American history, going back to 1850. The immigrant share of the total U.S. population in 2021 was 14.2 percent—tripling since 1970, almost doubling since 1990, and increasing 1.5 million since November 2020. The states with the largest increases of immigrants in that one-year period were Florida, California, Arizona, Wisconsin, and Virginia. Hispanic immigrants accounted for 61 percent of the growth from November 2020 to November 2021.

PARADIGM SHIFT

The Latino population surge has been the principal driver of demographic growth in the U.S. for over a decade, accounting for well over half of our national population growth since 2000. Most of this growth, by the way, is not by illegal immigration, but by birth! *Órale amigos!* Hispanics are now the second-largest ethnic group after Anglos in America. This means your son or daughter has as much of a chance in marrying someone named *Lupe* or *Luis* as they do in marrying someone named *Kimberly* or *Kevin*. Get ready for a little menudo in your Christmas traditions, my friends!

It is time to make the paradigm shift and integrate Latinos and other ethnicities into our ministries. *We either integrate or we become irrelevant.* To some, the previously mentioned statistics may seem staggering, causing anxiety and alarm. This may be prompted by fear of losing national or ministry identity or arise from a sense of inadequacy in how to connect with different cultures. What we should remember is this global demographic shift is a strategic part of our last-days commission. How we see it is a matter of our ministry paradigm and Biblical mandate. It is time we look at the changing face of our nation through the lens of the Great Commission. God is fulfilling His promise of a church that is multicultural.

These statistics optimistically reveal that reaching the nations for Christ is more attainable than ever before. In our generation, we can connect with diverse people groups while mowing our front lawns, grocery shopping, and eating at restaurants. We can preach and disciple people continents away through livestream and Zoom meetings. The world is at our front door, on our laptops, and on our smartphones. This is not to negate the responsibility to physically go to other nations and lands; it simply makes the going more achievable.

In his brilliant doctoral dissertation, Fijoy Johnson said, "Human society is ever-changing. It has changed tremendously both ethnically and culturally in just the last generation. Furthermore, upsurges in immigration and globalization are paving the way for a broader outlook on inclusion and diversity."[1] Johnson is right on point. We can consider the influx of people groups into our country as an invasion or a divine opportunity. We can focus on legal documentation or heavenly citizenry. If we choose to focus our eyes on the priority of our heavenly call, we'll see our mission is not as representatives of national governments or of a particular race, but instead as representatives of Heaven.

REPRESENTING THE KINGDOM

"Pastor Rae, this is Dr. T. L. Lowery!" He didn't have to announce himself; I would have recognized his distinctive deep gravelly voice anywhere. Dr. T. L. Lowery was a powerhouse, faith-filled, miracle-working, fire-preaching evangelist, author, pastor, apostle, and spiritual father to many. Always dressed immaculately in a black three-piece suit, with a starched white shirt, embossed gold cufflinks, and sleek shiny black shoes. He walked like a prince and talked like a king. In his 80s, he was still tall and lean, with a thick white head of hair, sparkling eyes, and boundless energy for the things of God. God had transformed his doctrine from one that espoused racial inferiority and segregation to a Gospel of equality and grace. In doing so, Dr. Lowery became the spiritual father of countless Black, Brown, and White sons and daughters who proudly carry his faith DNA.

"Dr. Lowery! What a joy to hear your voice! How are you and Sister Mildred doing?" I was delighted to hear my spiritual father's voice on the phone.

"What are you doing in three weeks?" he asked immediately without commencing with chit-chat.

"What do you want me to be doing, Dr. Lowery?" I countered.

"I want you to join me for a special service at the United Nations in New York City. I want you to preach to some of the ambassadors and staff at the U.N. Chapel with me."

I almost dropped the phone. He didn't wait for my reply. This was less of an invitation and more of a summons. He continued,

"We'll need all your information right away so we can get your security clearance through. I'll see you in New York."

Then he hung up! He didn't explain why he wanted me to go or what I should speak about. He expected me to find all that out in prayer. I stood there stunned for a few moments, and then shut the door to my office. Falling on my knees, I began to pray fervently,

"Oh, Lord! I'm just a girl from Tucson, Arizona. I am not the right person for this assignment. Speak to your servant, Dr. Lowery, right now and change his mind! What would I say to ambassadors and envoys?"

I was undone for days, praying the very same prayer, until the Lord broke through my dramatics: "You are My ambassador. You represent Me, My culture, and My government."

A few weeks later, I was in New York at the U.N. Chapel with Dr. Lowery, speaking to a group of ambassadorial staff and envoys from around the world. I was there as an ambassador, too—for a Kingdom "not of this world" (John 18:36)!

JOB DESCRIPTION

The Apostle Paul boldly and emphatically stated, "We are therefore Christ's ambassadors" (2 Corinthians 5:20). An ambassador is a nation's highest-ranking representative to another nation, land, or people group. As the spokesperson and envoy of a nation's primary leader, an ambassador lives in a foreign land to forward their government's culture and philosophies. This diplomatic mission includes protecting citizens, welcoming visitors and refugees, arranging visas for travelers, assessing needs and opportunities, and promoting peace between the two cultures. An *embassy*, which is the office (and on occasion, the home of the ambassador) is the legal territory of the ambassador's homeland. The ambassador conducts business within the embassy but is responsible to extend diplomacy beyond the embassy borders.

As Heaven's ambassadors, we are on a foreign assignment and a diplomatic mission on behalf of the kingdom of God. Our churches, organizational offices, and homes are the legal territory of Christ's domain, wherein we transact Kingdom business. Jesus said in John 18:36, "My kingdom is not of this world," and the Apostle Peter called us "temporary residents and foreigners" (1 Peter 2:11). We are Heaven's employees and designated representatives, living in a land and culture not our own. Divinely positioned as the Lord's emissaries, we are tasked with advancing the culture of God's kingdom, of which we hold primary citizenship.

Christ prayed to His Father, "Your kingdom come. Your will be done on earth as it is in heaven" (Matthew 6:10 NKJV). Our responsibility as His ambassadors is to extend and advance His heavenly Kingdom in the location of our assignment in the world. Our job description includes crossing borders, practicing diplomacy, assessing needs and opportunities, extending Kingdom culture, offering refuge and hope, and arranging travel visas to Heaven. Let's examine a few of these essential aspects in our ambassadorial duties.

Crossing Borders. Several years ago, Taco Bell used the catchy advertising slogan, "Run for the border!" This is a vital principle for winning territory. To be an ambassador, you must cross borders.

Human history is full of people who dared to cross borders. The conquerors Alexander the Great, Genghis Khan, and Napoleon

From Ambivalence to Ambassadors

gained new territory by crossing borders. Men like Magellan, Columbus, Lewis and Clark, and a host of other adventurers discovered new lands and peoples by voyaging beyond the world's known boundary lines. In recent history, courageous men and women have crossed the boundaries of tradition and prejudice. Nelson Mandela crossed over the hateful restrictions of apartheid in South Africa. Mother Teresa crossed over social norms in India to minister grace to the "untouchables." Rosa Parks crossed the lines of racial segregation on a bus and galvanized the American civil rights movement. They were all border-crossers.

Biblical history is also full of border-crossers. Abraham left the city limits of Haran to venture out with God into uncharted territories. Moses led Israel from Egypt across the liquid boundary of the Red Sea, and Joshua led them across the shoreline of the Jordan to possess Canaan. The greatest border-crosser in history was Jesus, who crossed over from Heaven's glory to our dusty earthen sod to win the territory of our hearts. Because of this passion for border-crossing, Jesus went to Samaria. Let's reacquaint ourselves with our primary text:

> Now he had to go through Samaria. So he came to a town in Samaria called Sychar . . . Jacob's well was there, and Jesus, tired as he was from the journey, sat down by the well. It was about noon. When a Samaritan woman came to draw water, Jesus said to her, "Will you give me a drink?" (His disciples had gone into the town to buy food.) The Samaritan woman said to him, "You are a Jew and I am a Samaritan woman. How can you ask me for a drink?" (For Jews do not associate with Samaritans.) Jesus answered her, "If you knew the gift of God and who it is that asks you for a drink, you would have asked him and he would have given you living water" (John 4:4-10).

In this simple conversation, Jesus intentionally crossed three specific cultural borders. First, He crossed over a racial border even though Jews openly disdained the Samaritans. He punctuated His point by asking to drink from her water vessel! Second, He crossed the boundary of gender prejudice by speaking in public to a woman, despite a cultural hostility toward women. Third, Jesus broke through the divide of religious pretension, exclusion, and elitism, becoming the friend of a sinner.

To be Christ's ambassadors, we must also become border-crossers. This takes intentionality and movement toward people who wouldn't ordinarily step across our threshold. Notice, Jesus did not wait for the Samaritan people to come to Him. Instead, He crossed over their threshold and went to them. He specifically went to the well at the very time the Samaritan woman would be there to draw water. Our text tells us she came at noon, in the heat of the day. Women usually drew water at dawn or dusk, not at noon. It is logical to conclude this gal was avoiding all the rest of the ladies in Sychar. After Jesus revealed her promiscuous past with six different men we can certainly understand why! I'm sure she was "persona non grata" with the women of the town. A gracious Jesus found her right in her hiding place. He crossed a border and went out of His way for a soul in need.

In this post-Christian world, people won't come to us anymore, so we must go to them. The early church's tradition of meeting on Sunday, in honor of Christ's resurrection, has sadly long been lost in our present societal drift. Many pastors, however, still have an expectation of people coming to us, crossing over church thresholds on Sunday morning. We have organized our entire ministries around this expectation. This tradition became culturally and legally instituted nearly two millenia ago by the Roman emperor Constantine. Constantine was converted to Christianity in 312 CE and is credited as "Christianizing" the Roman Empire under the ideal of "One God, One Emperor, One Church."

Whether Constantine was legitimately converted to Christ or saw Christianity as a way to bring unity to his vast empire is still debated. Regardless, Constantine favored Christianity both theologically and financially, advancing the Gospel message through his influence. He named Christians to high-ranking offices and organized the First Council of Nicaea to establish Christian doctrine and creed. He promoted Christian beliefs and traditions and endowed church leaders with funds to acquire property and build massive opulent basilicas. Going to church on Sunday became a key component and expectation of the culture. Ministers didn't need to go out and get people; the people automatically came to them. They, unlike the early Apostles, didn't have to "go," they simply had to wait.[2]

The world has vastly changed in the 1,900 years since Constantine attempted to Christianize the known world. People who do not come from a Christian heritage do not view the observance of Sunday morning church attendance as a necessity. On Sundays, they sleep in, have mimosas at brunch buffets, take their kids to swim meet or soccer practice, and catch up on their yard chores and laundry. So, we need to stop *waiting for them* and get busy *going to them.* Jesus instructed in Luke 14:23, "Go out to the roads and country lanes and compel them to come in so that my house will be full."

Practically, this means going to the people who won't normally show up at the Sunday morning Jesus party. These individuals may live next door, sit in the office cubicle across from ours, do our landscaping, or work at our local gas station. These people are our Samaritans, and we don't have to cross an ocean to sit at their well.

Assessing Needs and Opportunities. Part of an ambassador's job is to assess the needs and opportunities for diplomacy within the land of assignment. People's felt needs are God's opportunity to extend Kingdom culture. When Jesus ministered to the Samaritan woman, He initiated the conversation with her based on her immediate need. It was obvious what her need was, for she was walking to the well with an empty pitcher in the noonday heat. This lady was thirsty not only for water, but also for love (and a bit of relationship counseling!). Jesus did not stand up and start preaching to her about her sin as she approached Him. Instead, He connected with her over what she felt was the most pressing issue in her life at that moment. We know she really needed forgiveness of her sin and a relationship with God. However, Jesus understood that was not her focus at that moment—her thirst was. He went to the place of her need, the well, and initiated a conversation around that pressing issue. He asked this thirsty woman, "Can I have a drink?" identifying with her humanity, in that He too was thirsty. He then offered her "living water" that would never run dry. It's beautiful, isn't it? And so doable!

When our youth pastor felt led by God to transition to another ministry, I immediately called the denominational state offices and other churches looking for a suitable replacement, preferably a young couple. Strangely, months passed, and not one person applied for the job. While in prayer, the Lord directed me to a young ministry mentee. She was not what I had been looking for. She had accepted Christ only a few years prior, right out of selling drugs and running guns across the Mexican border. There was no doubt about her transformation, saturation in the Word, anointing, or commitment to the vision of the Church. She had been busily serving in my pastoral intern program and proved herself faithful. Yet I argued with the Lord about it: *She has no experience in youth ministry. In fact, she's never even been to a youth group, unless you wanna call her former drug dealers a youth group!*

She was, nonetheless, the Lord's choice. When I offered her the position, she was extremely reticent. Yet, under her leadership, the youth ministry quickly tripled in size, drawing kids from every demographic. Her lack of youth ministry experience ended up being her greatest strength. One late Friday afternoon, she poked her head into my office and asked to talk for a moment.

"Hey! I've been meaning to connect with you. Great job with the youth," I encouraged.

"Thanks, Pastor! I was wondering if you could increase my budget just a little," she asked.

"Tell me why."

"Well, I started this thing on Saturdays at lunchtime, and it's starting to cost me more than I can afford. I've been funding it myself up until now."

"Oh, I see. Well, tell me about it." A typical lead pastor, I was always wary of ministry directors who couldn't stay within budgetary parameters.

"I was at the mall several weeks ago and noticed a couple of Goth kids hangin' out at the food court. I went over and told them I'd buy them each a $1 hamburger at McDonald's if they would sit and talk with me. So, they did, and I told them I'd be back next Saturday, to buy every friend they brought a hamburger too."

"Oh, so what happened?" Now this was interesting, so I leaned in.

"Well, a few more kids showed up the next week, and more the next. And now every week more and more kids are showin' up. They've started coming to youth service on Saturday night too. But I can't afford to buy the hamburgers anymore. There's too many."

"Just how many hamburgers are you buying now?"

"Um, about 30 or more a week now."

"Thirty kids are sitting down and eating hamburgers with you weekly at the mall!"

"Uh, yeah. Is that bad?" she asked nervously.

"No, that's wonderful! Yes, you can have a hamburger budget!" I declared.

She had found a way to cross a border, meet a need, and connect the Goth kids in the mall to Jesus and our church.

In Luke 19 we see Jesus doing a similar thing for a short man named Zacchaeus. We find Zacchaeus up in a sycamore tree hoping to see the Lord pass by. Besides being short in stature, Zacchaeus had some significant character shortcomings. He had a shortage of righteousness, religion, and relationships. Yet, there was no shortage of Christ's gracious intentionality toward him. As Jesus is leaving Jericho, He abruptly stops under that sycamore tree, looks up, and says, "Zacchaeus, come down immediately. I must stay at your house today."

From Ambivalence to Ambassadors

Jesus reached Zacchaeus' spot—a place Christ had planned on stopping before Zacchaeus was even born. Jesus always stops at our "spot"—the place we are hiding, the place of shame, the place of sin, bitterness, or longing. He always stops where we really are, not the pretentious well-dressed and well-rehearsed place. He stops at our reality. He stopped at the Gadarene demoniac's graveyard. He stopped at the widow of Nain's dead son's coffin. He stopped at the Samaritan woman's well, and He stopped at Zacchaeus' tree. He found the need and stopped there.

That is what we are called to do: find the place of need in the community and stop there. It may be the spot of loneliness of neighborhood fatherless boys. It may be the need for shelter and food for the homeless. It may be the need for counseling and connection for blended families or single mothers. It may be a place for after-school tutoring. It may be a need for assistance to refugees or hamburgers for hungry Goth kids. If we will perceive the felt needs of people and then offer a solution, we'll have a harvest field greater than we can imagine.

The saying goes: "People won't care about what you say until they know you care." God cared so greatly about the woman at the well, He arranged for Jacob, hundreds of years earlier, to build a well so He could meet her need there. God's concern for Zacchaeus prompted Him to plant a sycamore tree for the same reason. Curious as to why our text in Luke 19 is so specific about the sycamore tree Zacchaeus climbed, I did a little research. Israel's sycamore trees are among the most impressive trees in any land. Thy have a divided trunk and wide lateral branches, which make them easy for even small children to scamper up. The sycamore reaches a height of up to 100 feet, with a crown spread of up to 50 feet. It takes approximately 40 to 60 years, a whole generation, to grow to full height. A sycamore tree was ideal for a short man to find a high perch to peek at a passing Savior.

While a sycamore produces fruit with seed, it has trouble reseeding itself. It is completely dependent on human assistance to help it take root and grow to maturity. This amazing fact reveals the intentionality of God toward Zacchaeus. Long before Zacchaeus realized his ill-gained wealth would not satisfy him; before he had a longing to see Jesus; even possibly before the time of his birth, God had made a way for this short man to meet his Savior. God had moved on someone a generation before to plant a sycamore seed on a Jericho roadside. That seed met a need and lifted Zacchaeus to see Christ. Here's the point: "Sycamore trees" are programs and ministries that meet specific felt needs, and lift people out of desperation. The role of an ambassador is to assess the needs and opportunities around us so we can extend the Kingdom culture of Christ's love, peace, and grace.

GREEN CARDS TO HEAVEN

In Arizona, the issue of undocumented people, or "illegals" as some tend to label them, is pressing and urgent. The largest percentage of undocumented people are individuals and families escaping poverty and drug-cartel violence. Their desperation is so great, they are willing to take the risk of dying of thirst and heatstroke in the desert, or of being raped and murdered by human traffickers. The U.S. government is not adequately addressing the immigration need nor effectively securing our borders.

The church I pastored in Tucson was approximately 40 percent Hispanic. The proximity of the church to the Mexican border meant undocumented immigrants in the congregation. This situation was distressing as we helped people through the agony of families being separated when a mother, a father, or other family member was picked up by ICE (Immigration and Customs Enforcement). As Christ's ambassadors, our focus was on their heavenly citizenship, not their earthly citizenship. The situation frequently put us in an awkward position. We decided to meet the pressing need and plant a "sycamore tree" for these precious and desperate people. We sought out immigration attorneys and refugee organizations to assist us in ministering to the needs of this population. We began connecting documented and undocumented immigrants to legal and confidential counseling and assistance. It opened wide the door of ministry to the entire immigrant community in our city. But holy tamales, did we ever get criticized!

"How could you enable those illegals? They are breaking the law!" some shouted at us.

"You are right! Our church is full of law-breakers. Breakers of God's laws and Arizona laws. We've decided to help them get it right with both God and the government. Why would you be mad about that?" I would occasionally retort in frustration. *Lord, give me more grace!*

Martin Luther King Jr. said, "The ultimate measure of a man is not where he stands in moments of comfort and convenience, but where he stands at times of challenge and controversy."[3] We live in a challenging and controversial time, and we must determine what our priorities are. Jesus drew open criticism and rancor because of how He treated sinful lawbreakers. The disciples raised their eyebrows when He spoke with the adulterous woman at the well. While not denying her sin, He still treated her with dignity. In doing so, He lifted her up lovingly into righteousness. He did the same with Zacchaeus.

Jesus looked up and said to him, "Zacchaeus." Jesus knew Zacchaeus was a cheat, spy, thief, and sinner, but Jesus did not call him by his sin, or the labels others had placed on him. A gracious Savior chose to call him by his name, and then by his destiny. Jesus told him, "I must stay at your house today" (Luke 19:5).

Jesus did not fear association with this wanton sinner; instead, He drew Zacchaeus out of his hiding place with dignity and entered his home. The love and grace was palpable! The religious were horrified and indignant, but Jesus is not in the business of bringing the sinner low; He lifts the sinner up!

Zacchaeus stood up and said, "Look, Lord! Here and now I give half of my possessions to the poor, and if I have cheated anybody out of anything, I will pay back four times the amount" (v. 8).

Something radical happened to move Zacchaeus from the sycamore tree to the Savior's feet. In a moment, this miserable, self-centered, conniving thief and traitor changed miraculously. That's the miracle of God's great love. It's transformational. It can tell an adulterous woman to "sin no more" and bring a prodigal boy back to sonship. It transforms a sinful Samaritan into an evangelist and turns a thief into a giver.

"All the people saw this and began to mutter, 'He has gone to be the guest of a sinner'" (v. 7). No! Zacchaeus had been a sinner, but now he was a son. Jesus declared, "Today salvation has come to this house, because this man, too, is a son of Abraham" (v. 9).

How valuable are the hearts of people to God? How important is their sense of dignity and longing for destiny? Are they more important to us than crumbly old statutes, dusty hymnals, and dead traditions? Are they not more vital than music preferences, service structures, organizational bylaws, and political positions? Jesus reminds us of this with a powerful declaration: "For the Son of Man came to seek and to save the lost" (v. 10).

We are here to do the same.

MISSING THE MISSION

Back in John 4, the disciples in Sychar were so focused on their immediate assignment to get bread for Jesus, they completely missed their mission. They were never there for bread. In fact, Jesus never even ate it! They were there for the Samaritans. We may miss the divine opportunity if we do not comprehend our mission. We are His ambassadors!

> May God bless you with discomfort at easy answers, half-truths, and superficial relationships so that you may live deep within your heart. May God bless you with anger at injustice, oppression, and exploitation of people, so that you may work for justice, freedom, and peace. May God bless you with tears to shed for those who suffer pain, rejection, hunger, and war, so that you may reach out your hand to comfort them and turn their pain into joy. And may God bless you with enough foolishness to believe that you can make a difference in the world so that you can do what others claim cannot be done to bring justice and kindness to all God's children.—Franciscan Benediction

Endnotes

1. Fijoy Johnson, *Can the Church of God Pursue Ethnic Diversity in Leadership?*
2. Rebecca Denova, "Constantine's Conversion to Christianity, *World History Encyclopedia* (worldhistory.org)
3. Martin Luther King Jr., *Strength to Love* (Beacon Hill Press, 1963)

IV. THE MINISTRY

*The work or service of a minister;
making and implementing decisions
based on policy and beliefs.*

11

Bricks and Mortar

"What I envision is knocking this wall completely down and making a great room, with city views out to the veranda. Then we'll demo the kitchen and move it over there," I said to the contractor, gesturing dramatically as we walked through the big, old, musty house. "What do you think? Can it be done?"

Renovating and flipping houses had been a hobby of mine for years. The house my contractor and I were surveying was constructed in 1962 on a hill overlooking the city and occupied over an acre of land. Time-worn and antiquated, the structure still retained its original kitchen, flooring, and confined layout, but it had great potential. It was exhilarating to envision the house rebuilt and refreshed for a new family to live in.

Building, crafting, and constructing is what God created us to do because we carry His DNA. He is the Creator and the Master Builder. Jesus declared, "I will build my church and the gates of Hades will not prevail against it" (Matthew 16:18 NKJV).

Paul called himself God's fellow worker in Christ's building project (1 Corinthians 3:9). In verse 10, he added, "According to the grace of God which was given to me, as a wise master builder I have laid the foundation. . . . But let each one take heed how he builds on it" (NKJV).

"We can definitely do it," my contractor informed, "but it'll be more than just demo work. To remove the wall, I'll have to call an electrician to deal with all the old wiring. I'll also need to fill in the concrete and patch the drywall before I put in new baseboards and paint. Taking out the wall won't be that expensive. But moving the kitchen? That's gonna cost ya!" he said, pulling out his measuring tape.

It is always interesting to me how a good contractor can take a vision for a house renovation and translate it into bricks, mortar, bolts, and screws. These elements are the unseen essentials that solidify a structure so a house can become a home.

When we began building a multicultural ministry years ago, there were not many church "building contractors" or consultants who could help me break our multicultural vision down into practical steps and tangible building blocks. I had to learn and build by trial and error, faith, and prayer. My father used to say to me, "You can learn through instruction or by experience. The latter is more painful."

Because I didn't receive instruction that was specific to building a multicultural church, I have a whole lot of scars that bear witness to my many mistakes, trials, and tears. My hope is the wisdom I've gained as a multicultural church pastor and practitioner will help you avoid my mishaps and form a blueprint for building your multicultural ministry. In this section, we will shift our focus to discuss what I suggest are the building blocks, nuts, and bolts that construct and stabilize a multicultural church. It is these unseen strategic and structural components that, when laid upon the bedrock foundation of sound doctrine, discipleship, prayer, and the moving of the Holy Spirit, make a home for a diverse congregation.

I. ARTICULATE THE VISION

Proverbs 29:18 says, "Where there is no vision, the people perish" (KJV). Habakkuk 2:2 tells us, "Write the vision and make it plain on tablets, that he may run who reads it" (NKJV). *Vision* is simply the ability to see beyond the point of where we are to where we want to be. It is the purpose for forward motion, the impetus for momentum, fuel for the journey, and courage to overcome obstacles that may stand in the way.

Joshua and Israel had a vision: the Promised Land. To an entire generation of Israelites, the Promised Land was a fantasy land. To Joshua it was a reality, just waiting for his bold footprint on Canaan's shore. Joshua's predecessor, Moses, had brought the people of God right to the banks of their promised dreamland, but fear and faithlessness dug their graves in the desert sand. Even after 40 years of waiting, the vision of the Promised Land still beat in Joshua's brave heart. Joshua was a man with tenacity, courage, and unstoppable passion. That is because Joshua had a clear vision of what God had promised and what he needed to do to attain it.

Even in the face of what others viewed as insurmountable obstacles like overflowing rivers, threatening giants, divisive factions, and fortified cities, Joshua remained undaunted in his pursuit of the vision. A God-inspired vision will make us and our people relentless, persistent, unwavering, determined, focused, and unstoppable. A clearly stated vision motivates and focuses. It infuses courage, creativity, generosity, and resiliency. "Vision will turn wishbones into backbones!" the evangelist Reinhard Bonke said.

For any endeavor, whether it be secular or spiritual, it is essential to articulate the vision or mission. It is especially important when building a multicultural church. That is because, in multicultural churches, people come from many diverse cultures, backgrounds, mindsets, and philosophies. They bring with them into the community of faith differing doctrines, traditions, opinions, and ideas. If our vision isn't clear, it will create a vacuum of purpose and identity. Nature abhors a vacuum, and the nature of people is to fill that void with their own agendas and ideas. Multiple visions are like two oxen in yoke trying to go in different directions. There's a lot of snorting and dirt-kicking, but neither ox goes anywhere. The goal is to rally people around one strong vision, bringing culture, gifting, talent, and resources into an aggregate agreement and a common cause.

A well-articulated vision or mission statement is an identification marker and rally point. It *defines* who we are as a ministry or church, and what our unique purpose is within the community we serve. It *refines* our activities and where we expend our resources. It is the tool that measures what we say yes to, and to what we say no. Jesus had a clear vision for his life and ministry. At the age of 12, He declared His purpose: "I must be about my Father's business" (Luke 2:49 NKJV). When beginning His ministry, He pronounced His ministry strategy, detailing whom He intended to impact, and how He planned to do it:

> "The Spirit of the Lord is on me, because He has anointed me to preach good news to the poor. He has sent me to proclaim freedom for the prisoners and recovery of sight for the blind, to release the oppressed, to proclaim the year of the Lord's favor" (Luke 4:18-19).

If Jesus formulated and articulated His vision, so should we. Here are some pointers in writing a vision or mission statement:

- *The vision statement must be Biblical.* Hopefully, there is no need to expound on this necessity.

- *The vision statement should be repeatable.* If we can't remember it and repeat it, it's too complicated for anyone else.
- *The vision statement should clearly articulate purpose and destination.* There ought to be a sense of motion within the vision statement, speaking to where we are going as a people.
- *The vision statement must be broad enough to engage diverse peoples, yet narrow enough to identify the uniqueness of our ministry.* Our uniqueness—not our sameness in relation to other ministries in the community—is what makes us valuable and desirable to the seeker.
- *The vision and vision statement must be repeated constantly.* This means not only weekly from the pulpit, but also in printed materials, logos, graphics, music, art, and design. If practice makes perfect, then repetition makes permanent. There needs to be consistency and continuity in the verbal and visual expressions of the vision. Questions to ask ourselves: Do our bulletins and screen graphics show people of diverse races? Does our building design and decor speak to ethnic singularity or racial diversity?
- *The pastor and ministry team must characterize, symbolize, and personify the vision.* Vision is not only what we say, but who we are. As our people see and hear us, they need to experience the vision. We must be the "vision incarnate," as must our ministry teams. So much so, that we are viral with vision, infecting anyone with whom we come in contact.

There is a lot of valuable insight and discussion in books and conferences around the differences between vision and mission. However, I found it sometimes gets too complex and cumbersome for multicultural and multilingual ministry. Trying to describe the difference between vision and mission to young refugees, for example, is daunting; not because of a lack of intelligence on their part, but because of language and cultural hurdles. It is important *everyone* gets the vision, not just the upper leadership. So, I've employed the principle of keeping it simple. I have come to believe the most profound things are articulated in the simplest and most accessible ways. For the multicultural ministries I've led, I've condensed things to a visionary statement and core values. Here are a few examples of vision statements from multicultural churches:

"Raising up a generation of culture-makers and world-shakers."—*Grace Culture Church, Phoenix*

"A global church making a local impact through life-giving ministry."—*Life Church International*

"Kingdom Culture exists to connect people with Jesus Christ through His love, truth, and power."—*Kingdom Culture Community Church*

"A multicultural and multigenerational life-giving, Spirit-filled church that welcomes unchurched people."—*North Cleveland Church of God*

"Saved by grace to live a Kingdom lifestyle of equality and love."—*Grace Kingdom African Church of God*

2. ESTABLISH CULTURE WITH CORE VALUES

When we land in a foreign country we become aware that the beliefs, traditions, food, clothing, and culture of the people are very different from our own. Churches and ministries, as well, have unique values and culture. Some churches have a culture of worship and prayer. Other churches focus on discipleship or make evangelism and outreach their primary quest. Some church culture is grace-filled and Spirit-fueled, whereas others are divisive, legalistic, and narcissistic. Healthy church culture is driven by deeply held core values based on Kingdom culture and intentionally cultivated by its leadership. Leaders are the definitive "culture makers" of an organization—the thermostats who set the climate and create the environment in which people can thrive and the organization expand.

Culture arises from a set of common values and shared beliefs. In a multicultural church, everyone comes from a different culture, and therefore different value systems. As examples, generally speaking, Latino culture revolves around the value of family; Asian culture values honor and discipline; and American culture prioritizes freedom, individuality, and wealth. In a multicultural church, we have it all! If we as leaders don't identify and create a culture based on specific beliefs and values, our people will be disjointed and vie for cultural prominence. We should celebrate diversity and honor differing cultural traditions, but we must find inspiration, direction, and solidarity in Kingdom culture. All culture must ultimately be subservient to Kingdom culture. Therefore, establishing corporate ministry values based on Kingdom principles is imperative to a multicultural church's unity, growth, and mission.

In John 4, as Jesus talked with the Samaritan woman, she eventually turned the conversation to the differences between the culture and beliefs of the Jews and Samaritans (v. 20). Jesus cut directly to the point and said, "Woman . . . believe me" (v. 21a). He was confronting her value system. For if she really did hold to the beliefs she rehearsed, she would have been living differently.

When we truly believe in something, it defines who we are, what we do, and how we live. Our beliefs and values shape us, focus us, and define our daily decisions. Deeply held values are convictions that slice through pretense and shatter the veneer of hypocrisy, touching our vulnerabilities and reshaping our identity. A core value inspires sacrifice, faith, courage, and action. Our beliefs and values are what create the atmosphere around us —our culture. To set the culture in your ministry, you as a leader must determine its core values.

One vibrant multicultural church conveys its core beliefs and values in seven culture-making priorities:

Our values direct our purpose and fuel our faith. They are (1) extravagant grace, (2) authentic faith, (3) Jesus-loving, (4) Spirit-empowered, (5) celebrating diversity, (6) purpose-driven, (7) mission-minded. This church teaches on these values consistently during their weekend services as well as in their discipleship curriculum.

Another multiethnic ministry relayed its core values this way:

We Are Committed to . . .

- *Reaching out and connecting with people from diverse cultures and backgrounds with the message of Jesus' love.*
- *Every person developing a personal and growing relationship with Jesus Christ.*
- *Equipping singles, families, youth, and children to grow in God's Word.*

- *Each person experiencing the power of God's Spirit and living with an expectation that He can do the impossible in their lives and others.*
- *Worshiping God with our praise, our giving, and lifestyle.*
- *Serving one another, our church family, and our community.*
- *Prayer as a part of our daily relationship with God and interceding together to see His purposes realized.*
- *Extending the Gospel to the nations.*

When building a multicultural church, *diversity* absolutely must be stated as a core value. Because if we don't personally and corporately teach, speak, and model diversity and inclusion as a primary ministry value, it won't happen. As with the spiritual characteristics of holiness and generosity, embracing diversity is contrary to our sinful nature. Diversity must be intentionally taught to be fully embraced. Life Church International in Atlanta, Georgia, led by Pastors Travis and Tina Hall, is a multiethnic, dynamic, and growing ministry. How they articulate, teach, and live out the core value of diversity is exceptional. So much so, I couldn't resist asking their permission to share it with you:

DIVERSITY—Since the kingdom of God is diverse, we think the church should be also. At LCI we intentionally cultivate a ministry that is multiethnic, multiracial, and multigenerational. (Revelation 7:9-10).

WHY IS IT IMPORTANT? Diversity is God's intention for the church. Whether individually or corporately, we'll never be everything we were created to be until we come together. In fact, the New Testament church was born in an atmosphere of diversity (Acts 2:1-12). According to Revelation 7, the kingdom of God is extraordinarily diverse and for God's will to be done on earth as it is in heaven, a church made up of "... all tribes and peoples and tongues" must come together as one for the kingdom of God to make its maximum impact in the earth.

WHAT WILL IT REQUIRE OF US?
To honor one another's culture. We are not color-blind. On the contrary, we see and celebrate the beauty of each other's uniqueness. Our various skin tones serve as a testament to God's unmatched commitment to beauty and creativity. (1 Corinthians 12:12-14)

To honor the generations—The Kingdom of God isn't just diverse ethnically, but generationally. We live by the premise that each generation needs the others. We learn from each other and grow together. (Psalm 145:4; Joel 2:28; Malachi 4:6)

To reject all forms of racism and prejudice—We believe racism and prejudice are ultimately manifestations of demonic influence designed by the enemy to prevent Kingdom progress, divide the church (and world), dilute the church's authority, and severely limit our collective impact. We love and honor one another. (Ephesians 2:14; Matthew 22:39-40; James 2:1)

To ultimately submit our cultures to the Kingdom culture— While we love and celebrate the unique nuances of our individual cultures, we ultimately submit our personal cultures to the corporate culture of the Kingdom of God; a culture of grace, honor, and redemption. (Galatians 3:28; 1 Corinthians 12:13; Colossians 3:11)

Pastor Travis and I share a spiritual father and mentor, Bishop Mitchell Corder. Bishop Corder has taught us, "Don't speak to what isn't there when teaching core values. Speak, instead, to what could be, and it will cause people to arise." Pastors Travis and Tina have done this with remarkable effectiveness. The value of diversity as stated by Life Church in Atlanta explains their success in breaking through long-held demonic strongholds of racism in Georgia and creating a community based on Kingdom culture.

3. KNOW WHAT YOU BELIEVE

In every church and ministry, it is important to clarify what we believe. In a culturally diverse church, it is imperative. People come to a multicultural ministry from all kinds of different traditions, and sometimes with downright crazy doctrines. As well, they may be brand new in Christ and still have the residue of worldly philosophy influencing their minds and hearts. In some cultures, there are indigenous superstitions mixed up with faith in Christ. We had people burning sage during prayer meetings, placing "curses" on government leaders, making rock circles in the parking lot, and selling divine healing juice and green prosperity oil to their friends—all in the name of Christ! It is critical we know what we believe, why we believe it, and how that belief manifests daily and practically in a life of faith. To be proactive, it is wise to post a doctrinal statement on our websites, as well as have it available in print at services. Teaching solid principles of faith and doctrine to all our leaders will assist in minimizing errant notions from having influence and taking hold.

If someone becomes divisive, disruptive, or stubbornly heretical, it is always preferable to correct in private and preserve people's dignity, if possible. This is a good rule for any organization, but especially when working with different people groups. Many cultures are honor or shame-based. Being publicly disciplined brings dishonor to not only the individual but the entire ethnic group, who in mass might become so embarrassed they cannot continue attendance in the church.

The pulpit is our greatest resource in defining doctrine and gently correcting issues that could cause confusion, division, and fear. The Word of God is powerful, dividing between truth and lies, emotion and the demonic. It heals, delivers, restores, and aligns. If we don't let little heresies rattle us, they won't rattle our churches any more than they did the first-century church. Let's just keep preaching the Word!

Hebrews 4:12 declares, "For the word of God is alive and active. Sharper than any double-edged sword, it penetrates even to the dividing soul and spirit, joints and marrow; it judges the thoughts and attitudes of the heart."

Paul wrote in 2 Timothy 3:16-17, "All Scripture is God-breathed and is useful for teaching, rebuking, correcting and training in righteousness, so that the servant of God may be thoroughly equipped for every good work."

4. LEAVE POLITICS OUT OF THE PULPIT

When leading an ethnically and culturally diverse congregation, bringing politics into the pulpit will blow up your church. You can do it in a culturally homogeneous congregation, but not in a blended congregation. Doing so on a divisive subject will provoke an all-out war or cause an entire racial demographic to leave the church. Politics by nature are polarizing.

We once had a guest speaker who was well known as a motivator of young people toward their purpose in Christ. He had effectively fired up our youth that weekend, so I asked him to minister in our Sunday services as well. Early that morning before preservice prayer, I sat with him in the green room discussing some parameters regarding the services. One of those considerations was politics. It was election season, and aware of his political leanings, I exhorted him not to bring that bias into his ministry time, since the congregation was diverse in political affiliation. "Just stay on message," I encouraged.

He was, however, unable to resist the temptation. He tried to whoop up the crowd, declaring one candidate as, "God's man for our nation." It fell flat as the people audibly groaned and looked over in unison to observe my expression. My eyebrow was discernably and definitively raised. I paused to see if this impertinent young preacher was smart enough to catch the clue from my body language, but he was not. I let him languish for a minute, while I considered whether my subtle disapproval was enough to assure my congregation of my disagreement, or if I would need to get up and bring correction. By the time he finally got back on point with his sermon, he had lost credibility and the attention of the congregation.

At the end of his sermon, I took the pulpit and clarified, "The opinions and politics of our speaker are not necessarily consistent with the values of our ministry." (At times like this, we must discern whether it'll make more of a mess by addressing the issue in the moment or if it's better to just mop up the mess afterward.)

In a multicultural church, politics will disenfranchise one group, and galvanize the other, creating division and infighting. In a truly multiethnic ministry, there will be Republicans, Democrats, and Independents all worshipping together every week. In our church, we also had refugees who had escaped civil wars, brutal tyrants, and civil unrest, so politics triggered trauma. Political persuasions and party affiliations had to be left at the door so we could embrace our Kingdom affiliation. Many ministers have a hard time with this principle because they have fused the

Gospel with their politics. Jesus refused to allow His message and ministry to be hijacked by political agenda, even though a few of His disciples were political zealots. Even with internal pressure from some of His disciples, a violent, corrupt government system, and self-serving earthly kings, Jesus maintained His missional message and focus. It is critical we do the same, and not get pulled off course by our giving base, influential church members, or our own political affiliation.

Multicultural churches need a strong consistent message of Christ's faith, love, and grace. The pulpit has the power to transform lives, raise hope, stir purpose, infuse vision, and empower for service. *Protect and preserve your pulpit for this purpose.*

On occasion, matters will arise requiring a Biblical, timely, and balanced address. It is critical in these times to consider the weightiness and prominence of the issue, and how it might impact the different ethnicities. Some questions to ask ourselves in these situations are:

- Will addressing this issue bring clarity and unity, or division and disenfranchisement to a segment of the congregation?
- If I need to address it, who do I need to talk to, and what do I need to read, to gain a full understanding of how different people groups will be impacted?
- How can I address the issue in a way that helps people see what Jesus is doing amid the crisis, and leave them with hope and direction?
- If not appropriate for a Sunday morning, what venue or platform should I use to address it? (I sometimes would write a position paper and post it on our website, record a short video for social media, or address the issue in a weeknight study instead of weekend services.)

At the end of the day, we need to ask what is more important—our loyalty to a political party and its platform or our commitment to Christ and His church.

5. INTENTIONALLY EMPOWER DIVERSE LEADERS

Diversity in ministry leadership enlarges our missional parameters, establishes our vision as authentic. Diverse leadership will make for a diverse congregation. Dr. Ray Chang, president of Asian-American Christian Collaboration, said, "At the most basic level, you know a leader is committed to diversity or multiculturalism by the diversity of the people they lead." If people of color do not see others who look like them in places of authority, and on our platforms, they will be suspicious (and rightly so) our multicultural vision is only wishful thinking and otherwise systemically unattainable. Some congregations pronounce themselves as multicultural, yet people of color are not leading in positions of authority, nor do they have a voice in the overall vision or direction of the church. In these cases, if people of color are only serving where they can be spotlighted, but don't carry any real authority, it is racial tokenism and not legitimate diversity. It is crucial that racial inclusivity is a consideration in choosing ministry leaders. I am not suggesting hiring by ethnic profile, but instead intentionally looking beyond our own race as ministry team candidates are considered.

We all have a natural tendency to mentor, position, and empower people who look like us, but we need to intentionally resist that tendency. A few years ago, I asked a prominent minister in my denomination why I was the first woman to serve and minister in certain areas. He answered, "Well, Pastor Rae, there are not many women quite like you.." At first, the affirmation greatly appealed to my ego. *That's right*, I thought, *I am one of a kind*!

Then the Lord flashed the faces of numerous gifted women in our organization before my spiritual eyes. I also remembered God's sharp rebuke to Elijah when he pretentiously complained he was the only prophet to speak God's word (1 Kings 19:14-18). Sovereignly checked and humbled by the Holy Spirit, I responded:

> I respectfully disagree with you, Bishop. There are thousands of women in our denomination of every color who are more educated and competent in ministry than me. They have been looked over and sidelined. But it is time we honored what God himself has approved and anointed.

What is true concerning gifted women is also true regarding the amazing resource of talented and qualified people of color, who stand by waiting for an opportunity to serve.

Some churches and organizations that desire cultural and racial diversity may have an absence of leaders of color within their present constituency. If this is the case, then we need to look outside our own ministry for racially diverse talent. Gifted and capable people of color are out there by the tens of thousands, we just need to "lift up our eyes," as Jesus told His disciples in John 4. This is not a matter of selecting a person for a position *based* on their color; it is, instead, a matter of intentionally *including* people of color in leadership considerations. When considering individuals for a ministry position, we should always consider male and female leaders of differing generations, and all colors and cultures who possess the 4 "C's" of leadership: Call, Character, Charisma, and Competency.

When possible, I personally prefer to hire and position leaders I've spiritually mentored myself. That is because they are already infused with our ministry DNA and understand our dynamics and values. One of the primary jobs of a leader is to mentor

Bricks and Mortar

up-and-coming leaders. Most of Jesus' time and energy was invested in training His disciples. For instance, His Sermon on the Mount (Matthew 5-7), was not a message for the multitude, but a "Discipleship 101" class for His ministry students. I believe in a "come help me minister" approach. It has been more effective than a classroom approach, turning capacity into competence while instilling our ministry values. Jesus employed this model with His disciples, which is evidenced in how He taught them to baptize people: First, *watch Me do it* (John 3:22). Second, *do it with Me* (v. 26). Third, *do it while I watch you* (4:1-2). Fourth, *go do it yourself* (Matthew 28:19).

Pastors Trevor and Adina Kring are a gifted couple I've been privileged to disciple in ministry. They began their ministry mentoring by driving me around to various home and hospital visits weekly, which they affectionately called *Driving Miss Daisy*. This was not only a great help to me but also useful in allowing them to observe how I ministered and served our people in real time. They soon progressed to assisting me in praying for the sick and homebound. After a while, I had them do it, observing and coaching from a distance. Finally, their ministry skills were developed to the place I put them in charge of the home and hospital visitation. They now co-pastor a thriving multicultural church.

Missions and ministry travel also give unparalleled opportunity to expose young disciples to God's indiscriminate anointing and power, as ebony and ivory minister together. More importantly, a regal identity and ministerial confidence are instilled in them, emboldening a "let's go there together" passion. We must have an unwavering commitment to cross-cultural mentoring, so people of color (and women) have an opportunity to build ministry skills and competency and serve in leadership.

6. REINFORCE GRACE, HUMILITY, AND RECONCILIATION

Misunderstandings and offenses happen in every family, but especially in one that is multicultural. Things are going to be said and done that will cause someone to get their feelings hurt and/or illicit angry reactions. So, be prepared! I'll never forget the Saturday afternoon that I heard screaming, cussing, and pots and pans clashing, in the church kitchen. Several pastoral team members and I jumped from our desks, and hurried to see what was causing the commotion. Expecting to witness a wild cougar invading our community area (it happens in Arizona), I saw very enraged women brawling like wildcats. Two middle-aged women, one White and one Latina, were in mortal combat. If you've never seen a girl fight, it's quite a sight! Even police back away from a girl fight. There was kicking, screaming, hair-pulling, eyelash-yanking, pot-throwing, and stiletto-heel jabbing, all in full living color. Their children stood in awe. I, however, was mortified.

"Women of God!" I declared as we pulled the women off each other.

"This is not how women who love Jesus act! What in the world is this about?" I demanded.

The Latina, with eyes still flashing in rage, was being held down by her sister-soldiers on one side of the room. She pointed angrily to the white woman, and wailed, "She called me a p***!"

We all gasped in horror. That is a very naughty and inappropriate word in Spanish.

"Why in the world did you call her that?" I demanded from the other woman, who was now cowering in embarrassment on the other side of the room.

"I thought it was a compliment. I thought it meant she was cute," she whimpered.

"Well, that is NOT what that word means! You basically called her a prostitute!" I explained.

She was aghast and ashamed of her blunder. After a heartfelt emotional apology, we were able to calm them both down and negotiate peace and reconciliation.

A good number of offenses and quarrels that occur in multicultural ministry are misunderstandings and blunders due to cultural incompetence and insensitivity. So, we included "Honoring Culture and Celebrating Diversity" as a topic in our new believers and membership curriculum. This teaching enabled us to expand people's cultural competency and instill the core values of diversity, grace, and forgiveness, into people's hearts and minds.

Some offenses, however, are not based on cultural ignorance and are not innocent in nature. They spring out of pride, superiority, and jealousy. If offenses based on racism, superiority, and a struggle for power go unaddressed, they become festering wounds that defile entire groups, causing rifts within the congregation. In these instances, we must reinforce the values of humility, servanthood, grace, and reconciliation. In a multicultural congregation, unresolved offenses can splinter the church down racial lines. The writer of Hebrews counsels, "See to it that no one falls short of the grace of God and that no bitter root grows up to cause trouble and defile many" (12:15).

Proactive leadership and a posture of grace and humility are key to fruitful multicultural ministry. Where there is pride, there will be rigidity in tradition, striving for dominance, and division. Where humility is exemplified, grace abounds and unity flourishes.

We cannot move from this point without addressing the fierce attack leaders of multicultural ministries frequently experience. Criticism and slander are unfortunate realities for every pastor, but multicultural ministry leaders seem to attract the devil's venom even more. I believe that is because nothing displays and demonstrates the kingdom of God more powerfully than diversity in the church. Therefore, the attack can be incredibly vicious, relentless, and, at times, very personal. As Jesus told His disciples, "Strike at the shepherd, and the sheep of the flock will be scattered" (Matthew 26:31). The devil will craftily use unwitting individuals to strike at the pastor like poisonous vipers to scatter the church.

Shortly after I accepted the position as lead pastor, a gifted couple who sought a position of prominence on our leadership team became disillusioned and left the church. Poisoned by their unfulfilled quest for power, they became disgruntled and retaliatory, systematically slandering me and our leaders. Fueled by deceit, they visited other pastors, contacted overseers, and wrote disparaging letters attacking the credibility of our ministry.

When this happened, two principles kept me grounded. *The first principle is not to take it personally.* Even though the attacks were intimate in nature, I had to remember they were not personal in origin. Ephesians 6:12 says, "For our struggle is not against flesh and blood, but against the rulers, against the authorities, against the powers of this dark world and against the spiritual forces of evil in the heavenly realm."

The devil and his demons are our enemies; not the people who are his unwitting pawns. Moses, David, Jesus, and the disciples all experienced slander and attack. They considered it a badge of honor—a sign their message and ministry carried the favor of God and was making an impact.

The second principle is to shake it off and keep moving. By the end of the Book of Acts, Paul had faithfully preached to people of diverse cultures and even to kings. In chapter 28, he survived shipwrecked and miraculously made it to the shores of the island of Malta. While Paul gathered wood to warm himself by a fire, a poisonous viper attached its fangs onto his hand. What Paul did next is powerful and instructive. He shook the viper off and kept it moving. Because Paul did not swell up from the poison of the attack, the people of Malta recognized the anointing and favor of God upon him, and the miraculous was released in their midst.

How we respond to the poison of vipers will either invalidate or authenticate our leadership. Discern and identify the demonic source, bind it with fasting and prayer, and then shake it off and keep moving!

As primary leaders, we do not have the luxury of indulging our emotions, carrying bitterness and offense, or allowing the fickleness of people's approval or displeasure to distract or sway us from our holy calling. Like Jesus, we must steady our gaze and secure our stance, keeping our mission at the center of our focus. Modeling Christ's grace, forgiveness, and reconciliation, even when attacked, authenticates our leadership and offers a living illustration to our people of our church's ministry values. In doing this we snatch what the devil meant for harm away from him and turn it into a weapon of victory!

> In everything set them an example by doing what is good. In your teaching show integrity, seriousness,

and soundness of speech that cannot be condemned, so that those who oppose you may be ashamed because they have nothing bad to say about us (Titus 2:7-8).

Next, let's examine those little things that fasten the building blocks together.

12

Nuts and Bolts

"Hey! This chair seems wobbly," I heard Brother Green exclaim as he settled on the rolling stool behind the soundboard. Brother Green was a large man with an easy temperament.
"Go ahead, Pastor, and test that lapel mic!" he said through the monitor. As I did, I could see him jiggling back and forth on the stool, testing its stability.

"Is everything okay up there?" I asked, a little concerned.

"Yeah, everything's fine. We may need to buy a new stool for me soon, though!" he chuckled.

Our first of our three Sunday services was soon underway. After the worship set and announcement video, I climbed the stairs to the platform to lead a time of giving. As I began, a loud crash in the A/V booth turned the entire congregation around. Brother Green and his chair had collapsed to the ground. Muffled groans arose from under the soundboard, as ushers ran to help him stand back up. In his usual affable manner, he waved his hand to let us all know he wasn't seriously injured. After the service, a maintenance team member brought the stool to me.

"See here?" he motioned, turning the stool upside down.

"There's only one screw in here and there's supposed to be four! That's why Brother Green's chair collapsed."

Little things matter. Below are some suggestions for the nuts and bolts that keep the ministry fastened together under the weight of a big multicultural vision.

I. IMPLEMENT A STRATEGIC PLAN

A multicultural vision is not realized spontaneously or haphazardly. It is accomplished with intentionality. Carey Nieuwhof says, "If you never get around to charting a course for the future, you will have no future." (@cnieuwhof 2/28/22) A strategic plan is an essential element that puts feet to our faith and organizes our leadership teams and resources to fulfill the vision God has called us to. A good strategy will minimize detours and expedite our progress.

A few years ago, I went to minister in Rwanda. I calculated the trip as taking approximately 20 hours, based on traveling in a straight line from Phoenix, Arizona to Kigali, Rwanda. It took 38 agonizing hours! I first flew from Phoenix to New York, then to Amsterdam, then to Ghana, and finally landed in Rwanda. Instead of going from point A to B, I went through the whole alphabet. I was exhausted before I even got there! We want to fulfill the vision God has given us in the shortest time possible, and with the least waste of energy and resources. It is important for us to know where we are in our visionary map, so we can chart a course forward.

When my kids were young, I determined to take two days to visit all four Disney World parks in Orlando, Florida. I had carefully collected all the amusement park maps and carefully plotted the course to my kids' favorite rides and attractions (or so I thought). The second day, in our third park, we ended up running around aimlessly, not finding our way to the rides. Sweaty, hungry, and frustrated, my son grabbed the map out of my hand, turned it around a couple of times, and declared, "Mom! You have the wrong map! This is to Epcot Center. We're in Hollywood Studios!"

We finally found a sign that stated, "You are Here," and with that information, my son, exclaimed, "We want to go that way," pointing us in the right direction. Then he added, "I'm in charge of navigating from now on. Mom's not touching the map again!"

Once we've figured out our ministry vision, it informs where we want to be. To get there, however, we must figure out where *here* is in relation to our desired destination. A strategic plan helps us draw a detailed map of objectives that breaks down our vision into attainable pieces and measurements of time. It charts a course from here to there, drawing the quickest path forward. Moving ahead in steps, and projects helps to motivate people toward specific goals and celebrate each success. This allows us to focus time, resources, and energies toward each step and ultimately accomplish the vision.

Without a strategy, your vision stays a fantasy. Some people think a detailed ministry plan dilutes our faith and removes God from the vision. This idea is not even remotely Biblical. The Bible is full of God's detailed strategies that saved Noah from the Flood, delivered the Hebrews from Egypt and into the Promised Land, as well as many more instances. God always knows where He wants us to go and how we should get there. Therefore, a ministry strategy is a document of faith—a written statement of how we have put our trust in the promises, provision, and power of God.

2. COMMIT TO A COLLABORATIVE LEADERSHIP STYLE

A collaborative leadership style is essential to multicultural ministry. It allows diverse voices to be heard, enabling well-informed decisions that best serve a diverse demographic. As well, collaborative leadership enables the all-important buy-in for ministry initiatives. An autocratic leadership style where one person, or a small group of individuals, makes all the decisions may work for ministries that are homogeneous in ethnicity, but not when there is the diversity of culture and race.

Collaborative leadership, or team ministry, does not imply the primary leader doesn't have the principal authority or the final say in decision-making. It simply creates an environment where opinions are solicited and encouraged in major decision-making and ministry implementation. In collaborative leadership, job descriptions, authority boundaries, and team values must be clearly defined. When this is done, it releases interaction, cooperation, and synergy among team members. If we don't lay this groundwork, there will be misunderstandings, duplication, and frustration among the team. However, if we've taken care to clearly define expectations, collaborative leadership releases a dynamic of creativity and mutual ownership throughout the congregation.

3. GET THE LANGUAGE RIGHT

Words are important. Psychologists have found our subconscious mind interprets what it hears literally. The words that come out of our mouths create the reality in which we dwell, for better or for worse. When language is used wisely, it can create a new reality, reshape identity, stir faith, and motivate action. Our salvation is inaugurated by the spoken word of faith:

> The word is near you; it is in your mouth and in your heart, that is the message concerning faith that we proclaim: If you declare with your mouth, "Jesus is Lord," and believe in your heart that God raised him from the dead, you will be saved. For it is with your

heart that you believe and are justified, and it is with your mouth that you profess your faith and are saved (Romans 10:8-10).

If anyone should understand the power of our tongue, it is we who preach "the Word." The words we, as leaders, write or speak leave a huge impact and create a lasting memory, especially in this technological age when our comments can be heard by the whole world. The words of the faithless ten spies were heard by God and created devastating consequences not only in their own lives but the entire nation of Israel (Numbers 13:25—14:10). The Bible is very clear about how words shape our future:

- Proverbs 18:21—"The tongue has the power of life and death, and those who love it will eat its fruit."

- Proverbs 11:11—"Through the blessing of the upright a city is exalted, but by the mouth of the wicked it is destroyed."

Most of us have preached from these passages on how words can build up or destroy people's lives, forward a vision or crush it. It is critical, then, we also consider this truth when choosing words to describe and define different people groups, for words frame identity. God framed His own identity using the words "I AM" to introduce Himself to Moses in Exodus 3:14: "I AM WHO I AM. This is what you are to say to the Israelites: 'I AM has sent me to you.'"

It is important that we get the language right when referring to people groups because our words define our and others' identities. Different cultures and ethnicities prefer to be identified by certain terms. For example: *African-Americans* or *people of African Descent*; not *coloreds* or *Negroes*. *Asians*; not *Orientals*

HE HAD TO GO THERE

or *chinos*. *Indigenous people*; not *Indians* or *natives*. *White*; not *crackers* or *gringos*. Many terms previously used for a particular people group are loaded with negative history and condescending undertones of which we may not be aware. For love's sake, it is important we find the terms each people group prefers to be identified with, and not hold onto disrespectful and disparaging old language. Frankly, it's "no skin off your nose" (as my grandma would say) to use the terminology and titles different ethnicities prefer, as they convey value and respect.

When it comes to labeling a culturally diverse ministry, I prefer the term *multicultural*, rather than *multiethnic* or *multiracial*. Some pastors do prefer *multiethnic*, based on the Greek word *ethnos*, which is used throughout the Bible. However, I have not found the term sufficient to describe the complexities of cultures embedded within each ethnicity. For instance, White people in the U.S. have many diverse beliefs and cultures based on age, economics, region, and family background. The same is true of Asians, Latinos, and African-Americans, as well as every people group on the globe. No one ethnic group is a homogeneous unit. Therefore, I use *multicultural* to describe our inclusive, racially, and culturally diverse ministries. Whatever term you choose, be intentional and informed as to why you use it.

4. CRAFT SERVICES THAT CELEBRATE AND ACCOMMODATE DIVERSITY

A weekend service should be an unforgettable and life-changing experience with spiritual and relational impact. No matter how small or large our ministry, through prayer, intentionality, planning, and teamwork we can craft gatherings that skillfully accommodate and celebrate diversity. From the welcome teams in the parking lot to the final benediction and prayer, weekend gatherings should communicate a love of diverse peoples and opportunities for a relationship with God and one another.

First and foremost, let's talk about worship. Music and the arts are the language of culture. If we want a multicultural church, we must be intentional about expressing the musical and artistic language of the cultures we hope to reach. If we are unwilling to move our worship experience away from a singular genre of music, we will *never* attract people of other cultures. We've got to be willing to infuse our worship music with the genres of our target audience. A cultural buffet of musical styles in the worship set is often called a "blended worship set" or a "blended playlist." It incorporates contemporary Christian worship with the specific musical styles that represent the various groups of people in our ministry. In our church, we blended contemporary Christian music with historic hymns, gospel, urban praise, as well as Latin rhythm and African influences. We frequently sang songs, or portions of songs, in other languages that represented people groups within the congregation. Putting together an eclectic worship experience that everyone finds meaningful requires a strategic focus, advanced musical and leadership skills, and a lot of hard work! It also requires a worship minister who not only understands the multicultural vision but is adept at leading people smoothly through blended genres, so people can experience joy and intimacy in the Lord's presence.

Warning: The worship segment can be the most thrilling and rewarding element of our services, but also the most criticized and divisive. As lead pastors, we must reinforce and model the value of wholehearted expressions of worship as Biblical, regardless of stylistic preferences. Teach the people how various music styles express the heart of different people groups, and that learning to worship to a variety of sounds and rhythms is an act of love and respect. This kind of encouragement will cause White and Asian folks to try to clap and step on the off-beat, and Blacks and Latinos to worship with traditional hymns and Christian contemporary music. Mostly, if you as the leader participate with joy in worship, exhibiting enthusiasm in the adventure, so will most of your people too. That means if we get our praise on in front of the people, they will do so too. Daniel Backens, senior pastor of New Life Providence Church in Chesapeake, Virginia, stated: "The greater effort any church makes in creating a worship experience that is dynamic, anointed, and eclectic, the greater the success it will have in becoming authentically multiethnic."[1]

Though music and preaching are the primary components of a multicultural worship service, the greeters, ushers, multimedia teams, and youth and children's ministers must also reflect diversity as a value. Representing the nations in your serving teams, platform participants, graphics, and design create continuity of message and authenticity of vision.

We also need to utilize technology to embolden and expand our ministry footprint. Background screens, lighting, and effects (FX), presentation software for sermons, video announcements, and a variety of other technological updates will bring punch and polish to our gatherings, appealing to a younger diverse audience.

We can harness the power of online services to reach around the world, creating social-media congregations. Today, if we're not on Facebook, Instagram, Twitter, Snapchat, and TikTok, we don't exist. These platforms are how this generation engages with us, so it is essential we utilize these valuable resources to broaden our audience and amplify our message. I recommend finding some young people to help craft a social-media platform and use it as an opportunity not only to promote vision but also to engage and mentor young disciples.

Overall, the goal of our gatherings is to reveal Christ, create an atmosphere where people experience the presence of God, and connect relationally while celebrating diversity.

5. PREACH AN ACCESSIBLE GOSPEL

The God who spread the stars in space, spun the galaxies upon His fingers, and likens our most advanced physics to preschool math, opened His sermons with such simple stories as, "A farmer went out to sow his seed," (Matthew 13:3). Jesus, the Word of God incarnate, broke down the most complex spiritual truths in a way even the uneducated could comprehend. When preaching to a multicultural audience, it is essential to communicate Biblical truth in accessible ways. This is not because a multicultural audience is less educated or less intelligent. It is because this kind of preaching is all-encompassing in its reach, regardless of race, social status, background, or linguistic differences.

Jesus told parables to animate truth and communicate Kingdom values to educated Pharisees and illiterate servants, all at once. Stories punctuate points and remain in the memory of people, because they draw on the imagination, forming lasting images within the mind and heart. Care should always be taken that stories, jokes, and examples are not culturally specific when preaching in a multicultural setting, nor that they are culturally alienating. The goal is to present the Gospel in a way that brings the Word of God out of the black-and-white pages of our Bible, into living color. In 1 John 1:1, the Apostle John related how the Gospel he preached was audible, tactile, and visual:

> That which was from the beginning, which we have heard, which we have seen with our eyes, which we have looked at and our hands have touched—this we proclaim concerning the Word of life.

Multicultural churches often utilize visual and touchable elements in their preaching. Illustrated sermons that include not only multimedia resources, but also dance, mime, orchestration, and other arts make the message magnificently memorable and indispensably personal. The point is to employ every resource available to us in making the Word of God engaging to our listeners.

Multicultural audiences are dealing with a wide range of complex issues. They need the Word of God preached in a way that lifts their eyes, raises their hope, elevates their dignity, and imparts critical life skills. They need inspiration, education, and a relationship with God, all in one message. The use of a preaching calendar is helpful in this endeavor. After fasting and prayer, our ministry team and I would block off weeks, months, and seasons of the year for specific preaching themes. This would allow us to break certain topics down into series for Sunday and midweek gatherings. By taking time to plan, we could cover certain subjects more comprehensively and target teaching to the wider congregation or more intensively in discipleship. Our worship and arts ministries would be tasked with complementing these themes with music, drama, staging, art, and advertising. At the end of a season of thematic focus the congregation, from adults to children, had an experiential understanding of a particular principle in God's Word.

Some ministers have expressed concern that a preaching calendar removes the spontaneity of the Holy Spirit in the services. I strongly disagree. God is aware of what He wants to say to

His people well before a Sunday rolls around. If we will do the spiritual work of fasting and prayer to hear His direction, we can present His Word with integrity and creativity. I have found I am more able to respond to the spontaneity of the Holy Spirit in a service if everything else has been planned ahead of time. Our gatherings for worship and the Word are His. He can "mess up" our plans anytime He so chooses.

6. MOBILIZE FOR OUTREACH

The church in Antioch, described in Acts 11, was rich in culture and ethnic diversity. Together they became the launching pad and funding base for many missionary endeavors. Their heart for the world focused their passion and energy in expanding the Gospel to people who reflected their own needs and cultures. A multicultural church has natural relational bridges to the community, as well as the nations, giving access to people groups who are otherwise unreachable. We can utilize these relationships and opportunities to rally people toward the issues and needs that touch their hearts.

Local outreaches which galvanized our people were: foster-parenting, afterschool tutoring, events for children in the community, teaching English, a food pantry, immigration counseling, and cultural immersion for refugees. Our international missions focused primarily on countries in Africa and Latin America because of our direct relational ties with the people already within the church. Many of these endeavors resulted in church-planting and significant partnerships with other ministries.

A church focused on its mission has vibrancy, purpose, and momentum. The people are less inclined to tear one other apart over trivial issues and more motivated to overcome obstacles and work out disagreements for the sake of missional success. A church mobilized for outreach lifts high the cause of Christ as its inspiration and identifying banner.

DAY WORKERS

The *work of the ministry* can be defined as "to serve, making and implementing decisions based on policy and beliefs." As leaders, our sacred service is to clearly define the mission, create a culture that arises from organizational values and beliefs, and implement a strategy that enables the fulfillment of the vision. However, when considering this weighty assignment, it is imperative to remember Christ alone is the Master Builder and Chief Cornerstone of His church. A career missionary, pastor, teacher, and author, Reverend Margaret Gaines, was often called the "architect" of ministry to Arabic people. She said:

> I wasn't an architect. I was a day worker. A day worker doesn't know what he or she is building. We don't have to understand the overall plan or how our part fits in the plan. Our part is to just love [Jesus] and obey Him. . . . Because whatever you are doing it is a part of the whole.

As day workers in service of our Master Builder, let us declare, "Lord, build Your church!"

"In him the whole building is joined together and rises to become a holy temple in the Lord. And in him you too are being built together to become a dwelling in which God lives by his Spirit" (Ephesians 2:21-22).

Endnotes

1. Mark DeYmaz and Harri Li, *Leading a Healthy Multiethnic Church*

The Final Challenge

We are in a critical moment in the church's history. It is a moment as paramount and pivotal as the birth of the church in Acts 2. That may seem like an extreme statement, but how we finish our Great Commission is as important as how we started it. I believe we are living in the literal last days, so our multicultural mandate to go to the nations is more pressing and urgent than ever before. The entire purpose of the Gospel is to reconcile all people to God and to reconcile them to one another. It is imperative, then, to demonstrate this marvelous and persuasive Gospel the way Christ intended—in living color, displaying the diversity of those He loves. Otherwise, it is not the Gospel given to us by Christ and preached by the Apostles. Until we collectively and collaboratively present an authentic and credible witness of Christ's body, in all its diversity, we will not be able to effectually finish our Great Commission.

The choice is ours whether the rousing chorus of the church's mission ends with excuses, whimpers, and sighs, or in a glorious and triumphant shout. We can stay in the comfort and security of ethnic singularity, or we can rouse ourselves and respond as Peter did in Acts 10 to the persistent knocking of Cornelius' servants. The world is impatiently waiting for a Gospel that reflects the complexion of Christ's kingdom and the power of His inclusive lavish love. The Apostle Peter awoke and arose from his dream, putting feet to his faith, and crossed the threshold into multicultural ministry to the Gentiles. It is time for the church as well to awake and arise to Christ's multicultural mandate. The distinct vibration of Christ's earth-shaking footsteps as He marched toward the old historic Samaritan well shakes us now. *He had to go there.* Passionately and urgently, He now beckons us to follow Him. Let us now, with steadfast gaze, unwavering faith, and unshakable courage, *go there with Him.*

> "How beautiful on the mountains are the feet of the messenger who brings good news, the good news of peace and salvation, the news that the God of Israel reigns!" (Isaiah 52:7 NLT).

Recommended Resources

Books

Building a Healthy Multi-Ethnic Church: Mandate, Commitments, and Practices of a Diverse Congregation, Mark DeYmaz (Wiley & Sons, 2007)

Gracism: The Art of Inclusion, David A. Anderson (InterVarsity Press, 2010)

Leading a Healthy Multi-Ethnic Church, Harry Li and Mark DeYmaz, Harry Li, (Zondervan, 2013)

Letters From Birmingham Jail, Martin Luther King Jr. (1963)

Multicultural Ministry Handbook, David A Anderson and Margarita R. Cabellon (InterVarsity Press, 2010)

Oneness Embraced, Tony Evans (Moody Publishers, 2015)

Still Off-Base About Race, Michael D. Reynolds (Kudu, 2021)

The Color of Compromise: The Truth about the American Church's Complicity in Racism, Jemar Tisby (Zondervan, 2020)

The Web

www.RaeOrozco.com